A

I'LL SET

YOU FREE

The Healing Touch

of a Volunteer

Wildlife Rehabilitator

By

Denise A. Ziter

1997

And Then I'll Set You Free

The Healing Touch
of a Volunteer Wildlife Rehabilitator

Copyright © 1997

Volunteers For Distressed Wildlife Publishing
First Printing 1997

Published by:
Volunteers For Distressed Wildlife
33 New Turnpike Rd.
Troy, New York, 12182
(518) 235 - 3981

**Cover Design and
Sketches
By:**
Donna Mariano

ISBN: 1-57502-619-8

Library of Congress: 97-91069

Printed in the USA by

MORRIS PUBLISHING

3212 East Highway 30 • Kearney, NE 68847 • 1-800-650-7888

Dedication

In memory of my father, Fred, who taught me that there are worthwhile causes to pursue in life, and that success is measured in the good that one promotes rather than the wealth that one accumulates by hurting others.

I would also like to thank my mother, Rose, who brought me up to love all creatures through her gentle approach to nature. She continues to inspire me with her willingness to share her home and her life with me as we approach our eighteenth year with **Volunteers For Distressed Wildlife.**

Donna Mariano, talented artist and dear friend, encouraged me to write this book. Her interpretation of the beauty of wildlife has made my stories come to life.

Their gifts are priceless.

Acknowledgements

Grateful acknowledgement to the Doctors and Staff of
Lansingburgh Veterinary Hospital
Troy, New York

Capital District Emergency Clinic
Latham, New York

The Animal Hospital
Guilderland, New York

For their compassionate help when
"The Healing Touch"
just wasn't quite enough.

The first printing of this book has been underwritten by a
generous gift from the good people of
First Albany Corporation
30 South Pearl Street
Albany, New York 12201

A **confirmation** of their continued
support of our **investment** to save our **valued** wildlife.

Logo by:
Joyce Van Amburgh
East Greenbush, New York

Typeset by:
Pauline J. Father
Schenectady, New York

Introduction

I decided to write this book because life should be a shared experience. What better way to reach a large number of people than through a book?

When I would recall the hilarious escapades of my volunteer wildlife rehabilitation work for my family and friends, they would always ask me if I had kept a diary, which I hadn't. They insisted that I shouldn't let these stories go to waste. I must reiterate the fact that this was volunteer work. You couldn't pay me for what sometimes seemed like insanity!

The true stories that are to unfold will not only broaden your knowledge of wildlife, but will make you laugh and perhaps cry as well. These chapters will be a new dimension in adventure, not in the typical sense of the word where the author takes you to unchartered corners of the earth. Instead, the adventure lies in my firsthand attempts to save birds and mammals who had been orphaned or injured.

This book embraces 17 years of my wildlife work, beginning in my early thirties. Yet I can't help but wonder when my love of animals first surfaced. My mother recalls her first glimpse of this love when I was three years old. My parents had purchased a new record player for me. One of the accompanying records was "The Story of Peter Rabbit." Mom remembers going to my bedroom to find me sitting in my little rocking chair with Peter, my tiger cat, beside me. Uncontrolled tears were flowing down my face as I listened to the part where the rabbit is caught in Farmer McGregor's watering can. I was so upset by this, even though I had listened to that record many times before and knew that Peter's life would be spared. I made myself listen to that story time and time again, never wavering in my loyalty to the rabbit.

To this day I can't watch animals in shows on television or in the movies. Even if the plots have happy endings, I feel that the animals have been exploited. To me, there is even sadness in their beauty and their innocence. I guess that three year old child still lives within me. Perhaps the seed of compassion was planted in my soul long before I realized what was molding my character.

As I matured, I became aware of the reasons why my life revolved around animals. A sense of duty prompted me to get involved. I have always respected the culture of Native Americans. I have lived by their belief that God created Mother Earth. He then gave us the gifts of water, air, soil, trees and the animals.

We were all given the responsibility of protecting these gifts, but our neglect as their caretakers is an insult to the Creator of such beauty.

There is, without a doubt, an acute spiritual uplifting each time I release an animal back into the wild. Surely there must be a greater power than ourselves who choreographed this delicate balance of nature. Since man's greed and arrogance have jeopardized the survival of God's creations, it is up to us to intervene in order to make right again these awful wrongs.

My love of animals and concern for the environment were stepping stones to what lay ahead. I had been involved in the legislative process through my efforts to get a law passed to mandate the teaching of humane treatment of animals in all New York State schools. As an elementary school teacher, my interest in animals carried over to my students. Faculty members, along with the student body of my school, Tamarac Elementary, helped local animal activists to get this legislation passed and into law.

Several years later, after having put paperwork and politics aside, I was introduced to wildlife rehabilitation work. With state and federal licenses framed and proudly displayed on my "clinic" wall, an avocation was thrust upon me that would both change and rearrange my life forever.

Join me on this journey.

And Then I'll Set You Free

Table of Contents

Dedication..IV

Acknowledgements...V

Introduction..VII

Chapter One
How It All Began 3

Chapter Two
Birds of Prey On a Holiday 8

Chapter Three
So Much To Learn 13

Chapter Four
Ready To Fly Solo..18

Chapter Five
Volunteers For Distressed Wildlife................22

Chapter Six
The Killing Fields 29

Chapter Seven
Horned Grebes - Eating Machines
and Hell Divers 35

Chapter Eight
Father Knows Best...42

Chapter Nine
Chimney Swifts...49

Chapter Ten
Premature Gray Squirrels 57

Chapter Eleven
"Please Don't Keep Me Hanging"...................64

Chapter Twelve
The Power of Positive Stinking 69

Chapter Thirteen
Anything But Wildlife 75

Chapter Fourteen
Momma Opossum and the Seven Dwarfs 86

Chapter Fifteen
Don't Call Us, We'll Call You 90

Chapter Sixteen
American Kestrel Chicks 95

Chapter Seventeen
A Duck of Notoriety........................102

Chapter Eighteen
The Bridge of My Discontent 105

Chapter Nineteen
I Kept My Promise 112

Chapter Twenty
Shorter Stories 120

Chapter Twenty-One
Crow Crow 128

Epilogue
A Song In My Heart 133

Chapter One

How It All Began

It was on a Saturday of Memorial Day weekend that I first met Marcia Kent. I had heard about her wildlife work several years before when our neighbor brought us an orphaned nestling robin. Our reputation as animal lovers was known throughout the neighborhood so it was not unusual to have animals brought to us in need of care.

We had no idea what to do for it, but common sense told us to dig up worms and feed the little orphan every time it opened its mouth. Little did we know that just the sound of our voices or the movement of the small box that it was in would cause the mouth of the robin to open wide. Needless to say, our supply of worms never lasted the hour, let alone the day! Then I would head to the four acres that we owned behind our home, with pitchfork in hand, to attack a new, untouched plot of soil.

That robin, now named Chipper, was soon the king of the Ziter residence, while Mom, Dad and I were his servants. We assumed the bird was a male, though at this young age there was no way of really being sure. The speckled breast would offer no clue to his sex, but it was agreed by all of us that Chipper was an appropriate name.

There were also three cats and a dog to consider in this cast of characters. Since they had always had the freedom to roam the house, some new rules had to be established to prevent a catastrophe. To make sure that the pets didn't come in contact with Chipper, we were all responsible to make sure that when he was **out** the pets would all be **in** and when Chipper was **in** the pets would be allowed **out.**

After about eight weeks of this lifestyle, it was time to set Chipper free. Though we had all grown extremely attached to him, our instincts told us that a wild bird deserved his freedom. Too bad his instincts didn't agree! Upon lofting him into the air, he made a giant U-turn and landed right back on Mom's shoulder. This happened over and over again. We then realized that our

3

abundance of attention had made this creature much too dependent upon us. So into the house came Chipper. Mom then went to work trying to locate someone who could help us undo the imprinting process that made Chipper think that we were his real parents, rather than just temporary foster parents.

After many unsuccessful leads, Mom contacted a friend at a local animal shelter. This woman introduced my parents to a couple who were volunteer wildlife rehabilitators. They offered to take the bird to someone who could help Chipper to readjust to the wild. They would pick him up in two days and deliver him to Marcia Kent.

I was leaving for California to take a graduate course, so I said my "good-bye" to my little friend, not knowing what would be the final outcome. I called my mother from San Francisco and was delighted to hear that Chipper was happy in his new surroundings, flying around in a large aviary with other robins. This was a good start. We were all hopeful.

Mom kept in touch with Marcia, calling periodically to see how the robin was doing. After about a month, Marcia called to let us know that Chipper had made a successful reentry to the woods that surrounded her home. He had learned the sounds of the forest, recognizing the distress calls made by all the birds living on Marcia's sanctuary and adjoining state land. The rich soil nearby offered an abundance of worms and the berry bushes were full of his favorite treats.

Now that our little friend was free, we had no further contact with Marcia until several years later. I had not even a hint that this woman's influence would one day change my lifestyle and my future.

Three years passed. One of our cats again came to the back porch with a young robin. It didn't seem injured, just ruffled from being cat handled. Rather than raising this little guy by ourselves, we decided to get in touch with Marcia to see if she was still taking wildlife. A telephone call confirmed that she was very much involved. The bird would be brought to her that weekend.

As holiday weekends go, I had different plans than my parents. All of my free time had been dedicated to playing tennis. It was the love of my life at the time and I was looking forward to three days of outdoor tennis. All winter long my tennis matches had been at indoor clubs. This would be a wonderful change of pace. But after an hour of fighting high winds on the court, my partner and I gave up. I came home to find my parents and our dear friend Lillian Deeb waiting for me to accompany them to Berne where Marcia Kent was waiting to take the little robin under her wing. I had a horrible headache from my tennis games. That made me less than enthusiastic about driving the 40 miles to Berne. This quaint town was nestled in beautiful mountain country. My mother was convinced that the scenic drive would do me good.

Mom said, "Take an aspirin and you'll be fine."

Dad added, "I'll treat you girls to lunch."

How could I refuse?

The little robin took the ride well. We brought a can of worms and tweezers, stopping several times along the way to feed him. As we climbed the winding mountain, we asked ourselves how difficult it must be to live in this area during the harsh winter. A four-wheel drive vehicle was a must. Finding Marcia's home was not easy, but when we finally came to her driveway, a wooden pole blocked the entrance to her forest hidden entry. A sign bearing these words greeted us:

"POSTED
NO POACHIN'
NO TRESPASSIN'
NO NOTHIN'.
THIS APPLIES TO FRIENDS,
RELATIVES, ENEMIES AND YOU.
SURVIVORS WILL BE PROSECUTED!"

Well, Dad wouldn't go beyond that point. Neither would Lillian and neither would I. So that left poor little Mom. She had spoken with Marcia on the phone many times in the past so she was the logical choice to announce our arrival. After crawling under the gate, Mom disappeared into the woods down a narrow dirt driveway and out of our view. If she didn't return in five minutes, we promised to open the gate and go find her. That would not be necessary, because within our designated time period, Mom came back with Marcia's husband, Ralph, who opened the gate and guided us in to his home nestled in the woods. The next sign that came into view said:

"DRIVE CAREFULLY
CRITTERS CROSSING."

We really had no choice but to drive slowly because their circular driveway was just wide enough for us to pass with the tree branches tickling the sides of our car. As we came halfway around the circle, passing piles of wood to be used in their wood stove and fireplace, my eyes became fixed on a dark brown log cabin. Chipmunks, red and gray squirrels, chickens and a rooster were scampering around while a woodchuck sat on her haunches eating animal crackers right on the Kent's front porch. I was fascinated by the incredible variety of birds at the feeders. This would be my initiation into the hobby of bird watching and identification.

Marcia came out to the front porch, where we introduced ourselves. We spoke briefly, because she was anxious to get our robin settled in and stabilized. The car ride had lasted well beyond the normal hour's drive, because we had gotten lost. The well–hidden driveway served its purpose for providing privacy, but prevented us from getting there sooner.

Our curiosity about the place was soon laid to rest, as Marcia offered to give us a tour of the wildlife in the cages and sheds up in the field just beyond our view. Every inch of the property was rustic. The natural environment that surrounded us heightened my sensitivity toward the animals as they came into sight. There were gray squirrels peeping out of hollow logs in cages. A cooper's hawk was nervously flying back and forth in its cage, within days of release. Next I saw a great horned owl who thrilled me with her hooting answer to Marcia's call. A sheep, goat, turkey and hens who were roaming around the property greeted us. A bluejay came down demanding a handout, while Marcia threw peanuts to the chipmunks and squirrels. Her apron pockets were always full of treats for these curious animals. Their only interest in us was the sense that we would have goodies for them as well.

We were then invited into the cabin where we found the living room and small den full of fish tanks with heating pads inside them keeping the orphaned babies cozy and warm. Little notes were written on the tops of the tanks to keep track of the feeding schedules.

Since Marcia was a radio dispatcher for the Department of Environmental Conservation, with the radios based right in her home, she was running back and forth manning the two business phones and the radio, in between feeding and cleaning the baby birds and mammals. Or was she feeding and cleaning the babies in between manning the telephones and radio? Well, whatever order, I marveled at her aptitude.

I offered to help her in the coming months since I was a teacher and my summer would be free to volunteer my time. Marcia told me to leave my telephone number with her. If the need arose, she'd give me a call.

I left Berne with a feeling of satisfaction because our robin was in good hands. Yet I yearned to know more about Marcia's work and my mind would not rest until my curiosity was satisfied.

We had so much to discuss on our drive back down that mountain. The Kent's isolated retreat had offered us a wealth of stimuli to pique our senses: the fragrant evergreens, the smoke from the fireplace that permeated the woods, the melodies of the songbirds, the hooting owl, the smokehouse up in the field, and the sun's rays shining on Tom turkey's glorious tail feathers.

This was a day to remember.

Chapter Two

Birds Of Prey On A Holiday

As luck would have it, the next time I saw Marcia was on another holiday weekend, the Fourth of July. The weather could not have been worse. Torrential rain combined with heavy wind, cancelled my picnic plans with friends. After spending the day reading, watching television and napping, a late afternoon phone call changed an otherwise dull day into a unique evening.

"Denise, this is Marcia Kent. Do you remember when you offered to help out with my wildlife work?" the caller asked.

I replied, "Sure I do."

She said, "Well, I just got a call from a woman in Saratoga whose husband cut down a tree and found several baby hawks in the hollow tree trunk. My conservation officer in that area is on leave due to a death in the family. There is no one to pick up these critters and get them to me. Can you do it?"

"Yes. I'll be happy to get them to you," I answered.

She continued, "Get yourself some beef kidneys to feed to them over the weekend. On Monday you can meet Ralph at his office and he'll relay them home. You might have to force-feed them, but don't worry, you can do it."

"Force-feed them?" I thought.

Perhaps it was some sense of pride or even embarrassment that prevented me from telling Marcia that I was scared to even imagine myself forcing open beaks and shoving down this organ meat. What about those strong talons that were probably ready to grab me? I didn't know much about hawks but I had a healthy respect for these vice–like claws that were used to catch their prey. It was too late to change my mind. I had jumped into the fire with great enthusiasm, but was now consumed by the flames of self doubt.

I answered, "I'm on my way. Just give me the woman's phone number and I'll call her to set up a meeting place."

After telling my parents of our conversation, my mother insisted that she go with me. After all, the weather made the driving conditions very dangerous. It would be better for the two of us to keep each other company. I still can't figure out how that woman's husband was able to cut down a tree in the midst of such horrible weather.

It was now five-thirty in the evening. I called every available market searching for beef kidneys. The last day of a holiday weekend left little meat on the store shelves and no butchers were on duty that day, either. We had nothing to feed those hawks, but our main objective at that point was to **get** the birds and then worry about their next meal. It was now time to head north to Saratoga, about twenty miles away.

The rain was still heavy as the wind tried to force my car off the Northway. This was an omen for what was to follow. As we approached the designated rest stop, we could barely see the parked car that carried the couple and the hawks. We pulled up next to them and I rolled down my window.

I yelled, "Are you the people with the hawks?"

The lady replied, "We have them in a box in the trunk."

We waited for her to remove the box from the trunk before getting out of the car. As she approached us with a very shallow box, covered with one sheet of newspaper, I couldn't disguise the look of puzzlement on my face. How could there possibly be five hawks in that box? If they were in there, did she actually think that one sheet of paper would keep them from jumping out? The four inch rimmed carton was designed to hold several six-packs of soda. Maybe the birds were dead. Maybe the birds weren't hawks.

We placed the box on the hood of my car, carefully peeking under the paper. There were five unbelievably beautiful young hawks, face down in the box. We had no idea what kind they were but their small size and feather development were clues to their immaturity. All this identification savvy was yet to be learned. To novices like ourselves, they looked near death! It wasn't until we learned of their nesting habits that this "cowering" is normal when birds of prey are sleeping or under stress. The movement of the box made them slide from side to side. Their carrier was less than ideal.

Mom excitedly said, "We've got to get these birds to Marcia immediately! We don't want to be responsible for letting the hawks die. They're so beautiful and we have no idea how to save them."

"But Mom, it's a seventy mile trip from here and fog is moving in," I stressed.

"Just take your time driving and bless yourself," she answered.

Every ten minutes or so, Mom looked in the box to see if the birds were still alive. We kept the car heater on low to make sure they didn't get chilled. It was a long trip up the mountain. We prayed that our memory and vision would not let us down when it came time to recognize certain landmarks and turns now obscured by rain, fog and the evening's curtain of darkness. Marcia's log cabin was a challenge to find under normal weather conditions. This night was anything but normal.

When we finally arrived, three hours after her initial phone call, Marcia could not believe her eyes.

She said, "I never expected you to come all this way in such horrible weather. Why didn't you keep them over the weekend?"

She took a look at the birds, identified them as American kestrels (sparrow hawks), put them in a cozy corner of her kitchen and introduced us to her dinner guests. We were perplexed by her calm, nonchalant attitude toward the birds. We expected her to provide immediate attention. Who were we to question a woman with twenty years experience? Here we were in an excited state, unnerved by the whole trip, yet she was ready to serve dinner and would tend to the hawks later.

She asked us to stay for coffee or tea but we declined, having left poor Dad home without a meal. I asked to use her phone to call Dad and let him know we would be home in an hour or so. Marcia sat down to dinner with her guests as we drove out of her circular driveway and headed for the closest fast food restaurant, about forty-five minutes away.

Marcia now knew that I was serious about helping with her wildlife work. I explained to her that if she wanted me to rescue and care for animals in the future, I would have to spend time with her. I needed to learn how to force-feed and feel a bird's crop to see if the bird had eaten recently. If I had just known that bit of information, then her apparent lack of concern for the birds' condition upon their arrival would not have been questioned. The kestrels did not need to be fed immediately, for you see, their crops were full and so were they! The humans in this story were the hungry ones. As long as the birds were warm and out of harm's way, Marcia and her dinner guests could enjoy their traditional Fourth of July picnic, albeit indoors this year. A summer storm system didn't stop us from our appointed rounds and it didn't stop them from sitting down to what looked like a delicious meal.

Coming down that mountain was the start of a whole new life for us. Bringing home dinner in a bag was the first hint of how our routines would be abruptly changed. It didn't take long to discover that we, as volunteer wildlife rehabilitators who use our home to care for the animals, would never have the luxury of eating on time again. Nights of uninterrupted sleep became the exception, rather than the rule. Nocturnal animals, like the raccoons, were easy targets for late night road travelers. If they were not killed on the spot, they were brought to us, no matter what the hour. If we didn't answer our door immediately, the rescuers knocked on Mom's bedroom window, demanding that we help them with the animals. All this upheaval, unknown at the time, was just around life's proverbial corner. First we had to explain ourselves to a disgruntled father and husband! Leisure time ceased to exist and the telephone soon became our nemesis.

Greetings and salutations were not the order of the day when we arrived home. Dad was still annoyed with us, showing little interest as we ate dinner and shared our adventures with him. He thought we were crazy. He soon learned that his patience would be tested innumerable times in the future.

At first, although not admitting that he approved of my wildlife work, he showed his support by building cages and allowing me to have part of the basement for a nursery and a clinic. He hired a contractor to build a full kitchen and made separate rooms to segregate the mammals from the birds. For flooring, he insisted on industrial tile so that sanitizing the place would be easier. White paneling brightened the basement. These were his gifts.

My recollection of his verbal support was after I had been interviewed on a local TV news program. I had discovered that several hundred birds were dying of an unknown toxin. The day after the program was aired, Dad was in a restaurant where the topic of conversation was my investigation of the bird poisonings. Dad listened quietly to what was being said. Then he proceeded to tell everyone that the young lady on the news was his daughter. I can still see him beaming as he told us at the dinner table that night. That's when I knew that no matter how much he complained about the hours of work or the emotional upheaval that went along with my commitment, he was as proud of my volunteer work as he was of my reputation as a teacher.

Chapter Three

So Much To Learn

I returned to the fun and leisure of summer vacation for only a week. Since Marcia now was convinced that I was serious about my offer to help out, she invited me to her home to spend time with her and the animals.

That particular July was a very warm and humid month. The temperature never seemed to go below 90°. In the woods where the cabin was shaded by the hemlocks, we were somewhat more comfortable than the folks in Albany, our Capital city some twenty miles down the mountain.

There were eight cottontail rabbits and five gray squirrels, all too young to feed themselves. Their feeding schedule included a warm formula administered by hand every three hours.

The American kestrels that I had brought to her were now joined by two more. The other birds of prey, the cooper's hawk and the great horned owl, were up in the large cages in the field.

The variety of nestling and fledgling songbirds needed to be fed every 40 minutes, so an extra hand to help Marcia would free her to tend to the barnyard animals that made up this wild and domestic extravaganza. After all, the hens had filled their cubicles with eggs, the goat and sheep pens needed cleaning and the turkey and rooster wanted their fair share of attention. Not to be ignored were the released critters who still demanded to be fed whenever Marcia walked out the door to the porch, where the woodchuck could always be summoned. His home was just beneath the floorboards.

It didn't take long for me to start my chores. I was shown how to mix a milk formula made of evaporated milk, water, egg yolk and honey that had been developed by Marcia over the years. The egg whites were not used because of a chemical reaction in the animals' systems, which depleted their bodies of a particular vitamin.

I learned how to properly feed the baby mammals, making sure not to squeeze the eye-dropper too hard. This might cause them to choke or suffer from pneumonia due to milk inhalation.

Cottontail rabbits were the hardest to feed. They were jumpy, scared creatures who could wiggle their way right out of my hands in an instant. Marcia was patient with me as I dealt with the first bunny who was chosen to be my patient. I had watched Marcia feed the first six rabbits, knowing full well that my turn would come all too soon. I had mixed emotions about the application of what I had watched to what I would do. Like anything else done for the first time, there was a sense of anxiety. I didn't want to hurt this sweet creature because of my lack of experience. Herein lies the great debate concerning experience. One needs experience but one can't get experience without practice. No time like the present to start.

A towel was placed on my lap. Before I knew it, the last of the litter was on the towel being held firmly by my left hand while I used my right hand to squeeze the formula out of the dropper. Several times that little rabbit nearly hopped off my lap. His quick jerky motions made it nearly impossible to feed him. If I didn't get some formula into him he would die. My body was so tense that the bunny must have sensed my apprehension, so I needed to relax my muscles or the rabbit would only continue to struggle. This worked. I was able to get some nourishment into him. I quickly returned him to the tank with the other sleeping siblings. Relieved, my attention would now be focused on the baby birds.

I was enthralled by the birds' instant acceptance of my introduction into their world of berry baskets and fish tanks. They were very content in the tissue-lined baskets that served as their new nests. When they were sleeping, I could just see the tops of their down-wisped heads but as soon as I spoke to them, they stood up straight and tall to attention, vying to be the first to be fed. This was certainly the extreme opposite of what had just happened with the cottontail.

The tanks sometimes held up to ten nestlings with each basket holding four birds. No matter how Marcia arranged them, the birds would jump into whatever basket suited their fancy. There was always a new seating arrangement each time we peeked into the tanks.

The mouth lining of each specie was a different color which fascinated me. That's what probably made feeding time so much fun. When they heard my tweezers tap the top of the tanks, their mouths would all open wide. I fed them in an assembly line method, trying not to poke their eyes or miss their mouths completely. I knew they were full when the chirping stopped long enough for each bird to stretch its behind over the edge of the basket and drop a perfectly incapsulated stool. Then they would fall asleep until the next sound awakened them.

The fish tanks surrounded us in the living room and tiny den. Marcia had either purchased them at garage sales or people had donated them. They were ideal for small birds as well as mammals because their feathers would not be damaged by the glass sides. Feather damage resulted from wire cages.

In the course of a season, cartons of facial tissue and paper towels were utilized. They generously lined the berry baskets to simulate a nest. A fresh tissue-filled basket was kept beside each tank to insure that the birds were always in clean quarters. It became automatic for us to transfer baby birds from a soiled basket to clean bedding after each feeding. The top layers of tissue were discarded and replaced as soon as the birds were put in adjoining baskets. Sometimes the birds' dandruff covered the top layer of tissue. This was a good sign because it meant that the youngsters were preening themselves. Healthy birds preen themselves regularly. This process continued on down the line until every bird, in every basket, in every tank, was fed and cleaned.

We then went up to the cages in the field to check on the larger birds and mammals. They were eating on their own but needed fresh water and a change of straw that covered the cage floors.

It was a great joy to be able to be up close to the farm animals as well. The turkey, in the field with the sheep and goat, loved to be petted and told how handsome he was. All he needed was several strokes to his head to entice him to display his tail plumage. It reminded me of a peacock in all its glory. This thrilled me more because I didn't expect it from a turkey. Perhaps it was the bird's way of thanking Marcia for sparing him from being the main course at someone's Thanksgiving feast.

The ewe (a female sheep) had other ideas. She loved to butt everybody who came within touching distance. She had a terrible pick on my mother. She would butt her so hard that Mom's knees buckled. It was the only time I remember ever seeing Mom intimidated by an animal. As I stood there, I chuckled to myself, remembering my last visit with my folks, visualizing the ewe and my mother staring each other down. Now it was my turn to make a wide path around the territory that the ewe had made her own. To my surprise, the animal did not see me as a threat. Marcia said that she was only aggressive toward shorter, smaller people. Marcia surmised that she was once abused by children.

Marcia had a "rooster stick" that she carried with her whenever she entered the barn. It was about five feet long with an L-shaped bottom. It kept the rooster at bay on most occasions.

The kestrels that we had rescued two weeks before were doing beautifully. They were in a large walk-in flight cage up in the field. They were eating thawed mice which they ripped apart with their curved beaks while holding the meat with their sharp talons. The fluffy down on their heads was now being replaced with new mature feather growth. I felt so good about being a part of their successful rehabilitation. I wanted to get involved even more.

It was lunchtime as we started back to the cabin. It was also time to start the whole feeding schedule all over again. Rehabilitators also need nourishment, so the quickest meal to prepare was open-faced grilled cheese sandwiches, homemade pickles and lemonade. Even lunch seemed to taste better up here in the fresh mountain air. We sat on the front porch stoop next to "TuTu", the woodchuck. She ate carrots, peanuts and animal crackers. We ate our sandwiches in between throwing peanuts to the squirrels and chipmunks who roamed the porch looking for handouts. Even the birds that had been released on the property returned for treats. It was truly a picnic among friends.

After lunch, Marcia fed everyone inside while I cut up berries and grapes. I also mixed dry cat food with a little water to soften it and then added cooked egg yolk for extra protein. The garden offered earthworms for the birds' diet, but there was always a need to supplement their menu with other foods.

Marcia went on the air as dispatcher at four that afternoon, so I did what I could to help her before heading for home. This included answering the many phone calls that she received from people with injured wildlife. When it came time to give them directions to her house, I handed the phone over to Marcia. She had exact directions to her place written on index cards. No matter where or how far away they lived, she could get them to her mountain hideaway. Some people were discouraged by the long trek. Marcia would coax them into coming by describing the beauty of the area and how it would be a nice day excursion on the weekend if they couldn't bring the animal right away. She gave them a recipe to sustain the animal until they could come. If they were totally against driving all that way, she gave them the option of meeting her husband in Albany and he would bring the wildlife home after work.

Despite the fact that I was so tired, having the long drive home did not deter me from wanting to make arrangements with Marcia to return in three days. I couldn't wait to see all the animals again. As soon as I came through the door of my home, I called Marcia to ask if she would like my help again. She was happy to have me return. Though my intention was to be with her two days a week, I found myself there every other day.

My only regret was that the eighty mile round trip was so long. On one such trip, I remember seeing my first scarlet tanager in a wooded area in the town of Berne. I had just purchased my first bird identification book by the famous author, Roger Tory Peterson. It was exciting for me to be able to record the tanager in the front of the book as I started my Systematic Checklist. Birders, as we are called, strive to find as many species on the list as possible.

On another trip to Marcia's, a yellow shafted flicker flew into the grill of my car. I immediately pulled my car over to extricate the bird. I was saddened by the irony of killing one bird en route to Marcia's to help save so many others.

On another drive up the mountain I came upon a community-wide yard sale in Altamont. I was able to buy several fish tanks. Bringing them home and cleaning them up seemed to mean that I was preparing myself for the eventuality of caring for animals on my own.

My chance came sooner than expected.

Chapter Four

Ready To Fly Solo

I don't think that I had been up to Marcia's more than three times when a situation developed that put me in the driver's seat, so to speak.

An elderly lady telephoned Marcia seeking help for an injured nestling robin that had tumbled out of its nest. It had very few feathers to slow down its fall, so the poor little bird sustained a fracture of the left leg. Upon finding the bird in her driveway, the dear woman was upset by the whole episode. She had no idea how to treat the injury, nor did she know what to feed this hungry, chirping orphan.

Marcia knew that I was just about ready to leave for home. She asked me if I would consider meeting the woman at a shopping center parking lot, not too far out of my way. I could take the robin home, feed it, make it comfortable and take it to Dr. Ed Becker, her veterinarian, the next day. When the bird was stabilized, Ralph could pick it up and bring it home. The Animal Hospital was in Guilderland, a suburb of Albany, and so Ralph was accustomed to this type of arrangement. I willingly agreed to the plan. Marcia handed me the phone to make the place and time clear to the caller.

We filled two paper cups with the cat food mixture and fruit. I brought along tweezers. A shoebox was lined with paper towels. I was now ready for my first wildlife patient.

The weather was very warm. At least I didn't have to worry about the bird's temperature dipping too low, causing hypothermia. As I turned into the entrance to the mall, I thought about how this vulnerable little creature was depending on me to save its life. As I focused on finding the car that had been described to me, I was able to put that thought out of my mind temporarily. I spotted the woman with her husband in a dilapidated station wagon. I wondered how they ever managed to drive there without falling out of the gaping rust holes in the floor of the car. They didn't have much financially, but their compassion and concern for the robin showed me how rich they were in spirit and love.

The elderly woman asked me if I would name the bird "Robbie" after her son. I said that I would be happy to honor her request. She made me feel very special with her praise of my willingness to help this creature of God. I wasn't the one who deserved the credit. I thought much more of her perseverance to locate help, after having made six calls to other groups.

"Well, precious little bird," she whispered, "You're in good hands now." She kissed little Robbie and handed him to me.

Her husband was anxious to tell me of the hundreds of pounds of bird seed that he bought every year to stock his bird feeders. He said that every kind of bird ate at the feeders. However, the pigeons were becoming a nuisance to the neighbors. They wanted him to stop putting out seed. He was determined to continue regardless of the neighbors. He also added that they were on a very limited income but were willing to sacrifice some of their own amenities to keep the birds well fed.

I examined the bird and found that indeed, the left leg was fractured. It would need to be taken to Dr. Becker's the next day. I gave the couple my phone number so that they could call me in a few days for an update on the bird's condition. We hugged each other without any hesitation. Being strangers didn't seem to matter.

I would come to know this bond between people of compassion from all walks of life. As my involvement with wildlife deepened, I was blessed with their friendship as well, for in many cases, the same people returned to my door with other injured wildlife. Many an evening was spent exchanging animal stories in our family room.

The robin took the ride well. His box sat firmly on the console which separated the bucket seats of my car. I didn't use the air conditioner though the temperature outside was 90°. The little one barely had enough feathers to keep warm. I opened my window half way to give us both some degree of comfort.

When we arrived home, I made the robin comfortable in our den. I put his basket in an empty fish tank so that the bird would not do further damage to his leg. I could tell that he had ideas about jumping out of the basket and I wanted to keep him from falling off the table. He could look out the glass sides and see the outdoors through the window, taking in the morning sunshine which was vital to his bone development.

I was up bright and early the next morning eager to see if Robbie had survived the night. There he was, responding to the opening of the den's squeaky sliding door. He opened his mouth wide, demanding breakfast. He tried to balance himself on his one good leg. His wings acted as crutches. I hadn't brought the food in with me which was a big mistake. I rushed back to the kitchen to soak the dry cat food. I had cut up fruit the night before so that was what I gave him until the cat food had softened. Robbie was quite the eater. I filled his mouth five times before he seemed full. I waited for his little "gift" to be deposited over the side of the basket. Then it was time for him to take a short snooze. This would be repeated every half hour.

After calling Dr. Becker's office to make an appointment, I did the usual household chores. It was a constant temptation to stop my mundane housework, choosing instead to visit with Robbie. Yet I knew from my visits with Marcia that any noises would excite the bird enough to initiate another feeding that was not scheduled. It didn't matter that he had just been fed five minutes earlier.

In late morning, we left for Dr. Becker's hospital. It was a 45 minute ride. Robbie was now becoming a seasoned traveler. The receptionist was expecting us. She asked me all sorts of questions about the bird, recording everything on an index card. I had to leave Robbie there overnight because the doctor treated wildlife in between his regular patients. I was told to call late in the afternoon to see if the bird could be saved. I would have to wait until then to find out whether I could return the next day to bring Robbie home. I missed my chirping friend on the ride back to Troy.

The woman called that evening to check on Robbie's progress. I could tell from her voice that she was hesitant to ask if the bird was still alive. I was happy to report that the doctor had set Robbie's leg and I could bring him home the next morning. The healing process would take about three weeks, with a return visit to the clinic in seven days to check the cast. She was overjoyed.

She called periodically to check on Robbie. Our conversations also covered many other topics as well. As the weeks passed, the calls became less frequent. Our last chat was when the robin was released on Marcia's property. I called to tell her the good news. She was so grateful for the seven weeks of care that I had given the bird. The leg had healed nicely. I waited until he was full grown to bring him to Marcia's, where he stayed in an outside aviary to adjust to the surroundings.

Release day was exciting for me. I drove to Berne to spend my day helping Marcia. It had to be on a Saturday because I was back teaching second grade. Robbie was flying around the aviary with many other robins. You could sense their restlessness. I opened the door of the cage and spoke gently, encouraging them all to grab the moment and fly to freedom. They knew just what to do. They flew out the door, gained altitude with little effort and reached the treetops. Robbie flicked his tail as he perched so proudly in a maple tree. His cage buddies called to him and he responded by joining them in the trees that bordered the field. I couldn't help but feel great satisfaction. In fact, the taste of his success was addictive. As Marcia and I walked back to the porch, she assured me that I would see Robbie at least several more times. The newly released birds always came to the porch for food, waiting for mealworms to be tossed to the ground for them. Gradually, they would instinctively leave the property to begin lives of complete wildness.

I never heard from my lady friend after that last phone call. The rescue mission had reached a successful conclusion. Many hands, but a common goal, had brought strangers together to save one little bird's life. No life is insignificant. Maybe that's the secret that needs to be shared by more people in this complicated, technical world of ours. Robbie, and all the others who were fed by that couple, gave them a purpose in life. He gave them the opportunity to have many warm conversations with a stranger. He gave me my first rehabilitation experience and he was a wild patient in a world of domestic veterinary care. Now Robbie was free to give back to nature what only he and his kind can give her: balance and beauty and the promise of springtime.

Chapter Five

Volunteers For Distressed Wildlife

I discovered very quickly that the public wasn't always pleasant. One afternoon, after leaving another bird at Dr. Becker's office, I no sooner came in the door when the phone rang. When a man asked for me and mispronounced my name, I thought it was the veterinarian calling me directly rather than having his receptionist do it. It was not the doctor. Instead, it was a very arrogant man who demanded my immediate help for an injured American kestrel.

He started, "I have called six other people on the list. They either don't answer or can't help me so if **you** don't help me, I'll just drown this hawk in my sink!"

I said, "Where are you located?"

"Inner city Albany," he replied.

"There's a Dr. Ed Becker in Guilderland who will take a look at the hawk for you," I advised.

"Lady, this bird fell out of the sky. It ain't my bird! You expect me to take it to a vet? And besides, I'm a leg man," he said sarcastically.

I asked, "What do you mean you're a leg man?"

"I don't drive. I walk. I get fresh air, man," he quipped.

In the background I could hear the "killy-killying" noises that a kestrel makes as well as the voices of several other people carrying on and laughing.

I asked, "What do you have the bird in?"

"A basket," he answered.

"The hawk should be kept in a covered box where it's dark and quiet," I said firmly.

"Lady, if you don't come here and get this thing, I'll drown it, wrap it up in newspaper and send it over to you," he threatened.

"Just calm down. Since you do not have a box, I'll bring a carrier with me," I said.

He retorted, "Oh you mean like an aircraft carrier?"

"No. Like a cat carrier," I answered patiently.

"Thirty minutes," I added.

"Well, get a lead foot and be here in fifteen minutes. I'm in a hurry," he demanded.

"Listen buddy. I'm not going to take your rudeness any longer." With that, I slammed down the receiver. Boy, was I shaken. I could feel my temples pulsating as my blood pressure rose. I was angry at him yet concerned for the hawk's safety. Had my actions set into motion this man's threat?

I started toward the kitchen to tell my mother of the upsetting conversation when the phone rang again. I thought for sure that it was that obnoxious character calling back to have the last word. Being the brave person that I was, I had my mother answer the call! Fortunately, for her sake as well as mine, it was Marcia. She had gotten a phone call from the same guy not ten minutes before I had. He had been just as impertinent with her. She had explained to him that she did not drive and couldn't pick up the bird. She also advised him to take the kestrel to Dr. Becker. After getting no satisfaction from her, he proceeded to dial my number. I told her how badly I felt about losing my cool. I had tried so hard to remain unfazed by his attitude but there was a limit to how much verbal abuse I would allow. Marcia told me to chalk it up to experience. Besides, it wouldn't have been wise to go to that section of Albany by myself, walking into an unknown set of circumstances that could jeopardize my safety. That guy and his friends could have very likely been high on alcohol or drugs.

Well, the story does have a happy ending. The caller tried one more name on his list. Where this so-called list came from is unknown but he contacted Fraya Katz, a rehabilitator who lived four blocks from where he lived. He played out the same wise-cracking scenario. However, this time Fraya managed to persuade him to walk to her house with the kestrel wrapped in his jacket. The bird was not injured. It was very young and needed time for the primary feathers to complete their growth.

Fraya called Marcia to see if she could relay the kestrel to her via Ralph. This was an arrangement to which Ralph had become accustomed. Fraya held her wildlife temporarily until she could transfer them to Marcia. Ralph always seemed to have animals in his truck to keep him company on his way home.

Unloading bags of groceries **and** boxes of critters became routine for him once he arrived at their log cabin.

The kestrel, despite its shaky start, had a wonderful life with Marcia, housed with others of his kind and able to be released within four weeks of arrival. The area was adjacent to hundreds of acres of state land. There was an abundance of natural food for all the animals that were released on Marcia's property.

Before the summer was over, I had applied for my own rehabilitator's license from the New York State Department of Environmental Conservation. It was also necessary for me to apply for a federal migratory bird permit. I had been working under Marcia's license but that was only temporary, since I would always bring the animals to her for the final stage of their rehabilitation. There seemed to be something missing, because I was not afforded the full responsibility of the animals' care.

At that same time, Marcia thought it would be beneficial for me to meet the two other local women who had also recently obtained their permits. Mom and I met them for lunch at Marcia's. We got to know each other on a personal level as well as shared our new found enthusiasm for this wildlife hobby. It was a good time to jot down everyone's telephone numbers and directions to their homes, because we were sure that this was not our last get-together. In fact, out of this initial visit, a tax-exempt organization called Volunteers For Distressed Wildlife was formed. Marcia now had people willing to share her load. Marylou Riccardo, Fraya Katz, Mom, Marcia and I were the founding members. As the years went by, associate members were voted into the group. They would assist us in many different ways.

It seemed like forever before we gained our non–profit status. Fraya was credited with having the knowledge to accomplish this task. An attorney in her family guided her through the bureaucratic maze of paperwork. We were happy to pass this responsibility on to her.

We were not without our own responsibilities. Marylou started a checking account with the $25.^{00} that we each agreed to pay. She established credit with mail-order companies in order to purchase the many supplies that we would need to get the organization on its feet.

Marcia typed up our Constitution and By-Laws after we had met for a second time to discuss our purpose and goals. She also wrote letters to companies seeking donations of money or goods to help us get started.

My responsibilities were to purchase medications, take the minutes of our meetings, write corporate grant applications and produce a brochure.

Mom made phone calls to local stores, asking for their help. She assumed all my rehabilitation duties while I was at work. She willingly answered all the wildlife calls.

Every penny spent for our volunteer work came out of our own pockets for at least the first year. Once in a while, a client made a donation after having dropped off an animal at our door. The ironic part was that most people thought that we all worked for the Conservation Department. They were under the false impression that we were all well paid state workers. The Conservation Department was certainly given too much credit, since its only connection to us was the issuance of our licenses once a year. Wildlife rehabilitation was certainly not a priority for the state. Private citizens, such as ourselves, found it necessary to take matters into their own hands when it came to saving wildlife.

Our only relief from the state came in the form of our tax-exempt status. Everything we needed was taxable, so we were lucky to have finally received notice of our application being accepted after many revisions and resubmissions. We were now out of the starting gate, off and running.

Marcia received information in the mail regarding a seminar that was going to be held at Cornell in Ithaca. It would be a three day series of lectures for rehabilitators, veterinarians and anyone interested in wildlife conservation. When she asked me if I was interested in attending, I jumped at the opportunity to go. We made hotel reservations and sent in our applications and registration fees to Cornell.

Marylou stayed home to care for our animals. Fraya would meet us in Ithaca on Saturday, the second day of the seminar.

The day was beautiful for the four hour trip to the campus. I drove while Marcia acted as my navigator. Several hours into the ride we became involved in an animal rescue. A little gray poodle was running down the center lane of a country road where the speed limit was 55 mph. It was a stretch of highway with mostly farm land and one solitary house to our right. Without saying a word to each other, our instincts to save this wayward pooch jumped into action. I pulled the car over to the shoulder. I looked in my rearview mirror only to see cars approaching us from about a quarter mile away. The poodle was acting confused and scared so we whistled to him as we exited the car. We walked toward a field, hoping to coax the dog out of the road. The dog had no intention of coming near us. Instead, he ran toward the house and began barking at us as if we were unwelcome intruders on his property! We returned to the car, laughing at ourselves for letting this dog make us look like fools. We were relieved that we didn't witness the dog's demise and happy that we didn't have to take this poodle along with us to Cornell.

After we were settled into our room, we registered at the university. We then visited a wildlife refuge owned by Cornell called Sapsucker Woods. I knew very little about birds, so it was fun being with someone who could point out the sounds and surroundings that made birdwatching so interesting.

The Visitor's Center had huge plate glass windows overlooking several ponds full of different species of ducks. Well-hidden speakers placed around the ponds allowed us to hear birds as if we were outside. Bird feeders around the perimeter of the building were frequented by all kinds of songbirds, as well as chipmunks and squirrels.

The gift shop was a bird lover's delight. Every type of book, slide and poster was available. We parted with a large amount of our spending money there.

We then toured a display of stuffed birds, including a large collection of hummingbirds from all over the world. They certainly were a stark contrast to the active, noisy birds that we had left back home with Mom and Marylou.

The rest of the weekend was spent attending lectures. I can't say that I learned much, since many of the discussions were way over my head as a beginner. I did meet people whom I would come to know at future seminars, sharing ideas and contacting each other when we needed specific questions answered. Some rehabilitators specialized in birds of prey, while others preferred just to do raccoons or deer. Volunteers For Distressed Wildlife members cared for small mammals, deer and all types of birds, including raptors. I had my work cut out for me, having to learn from the ground up about every one of these animals.

Fraya arrived on Saturday. She had made arrangements in advance to meet with several veterinarians and wildlife researchers to discuss a cataract problem that had developed in her raccoons. Young raccoons with poor vision, leading to blindness, were probably the result of an incorrect feeding formula.

Since this condition was exhibiting itself throughout the rehabilitation community, Cornell was the best place to have the raccoons examined.

In 1980, wildlife rehabilitation in New York State was in its infancy. There were always people who helped wildlife, quietly and single handedly, like the farmer who treated a fawn injured or orphaned on his land; the pet owner whose cat or dog had caught a baby bird or squirrel; the homeowner who found a baby raccoon in his attic, wanting to raise it and keep it for a pet. Whatever the motives, these people usually cared for the animals with little knowledge about the proper diets or housing requirements so the animals were ill-equipped for release back into the wild. Some were kept as house pets, while most died. Now people were beginning to be licensed and regulated. Organizations such as ours were forming all over the state to join forces to save wildlife. The state could no longer ignore us. We were looked upon as a necessary evil. Since wildlife rehabilitation was not a top Conservation Department priority and private citizens were willing to donate their time and money to volunteer, we no longer could be overlooked. Instead, wildlife rehabilitation was now regulated by the state. All volunteers were required to send in detailed logs of our daily activities. At the end of the year, in order to have our permits renewed, we would send in these pages of logs. Soon after, if our logs were accepted, a new permit would be sent to us with updated regulations, usually full of new limitations and questionable doctrine. Common sense was never the order of the day.

Inspections of our facilities were possible, but budget constraints always seemed to be the perfect excuse for not performing these important duties. How would the state ever know what these 400 volunteers were doing without visiting their homes and wildlife centers? Just because we were eventually required to pass a test to become licensed did not mean that the animals were in clean quarters or fed properly or kept in cages large enough for the animals to exercise their muscles and strengthen their bones. I had been horrified to see the living conditions under which some poor wild animals had been kept. These so-called rehabilitators should have been arrested for animal abuse, rather than have been given licenses. This was why inspections were so vital. Passing an exam that was administered by the Conservation Department did not make us qualified to be good rehabilitators. Seminars such as the one we were attending offered a foundation on which to build our expertise. More important, we needed to put into practice what we had learned, as well as give the animals clean, well designed cages and aviaries. The least amount of stress afforded the animals a much better chance for their survival.

Fraya was a conscientious rehaber. She was willing to drive all the way to Ithaca to take her raccoon to be examined by the experts. It was determined that the Espilac puppy formula that had been the recommended commercial formula for raccoons, was now suspected of being the cause of the cataracts. Since the female specie of each mammal has her own unique type of milk, it is difficult to duplicate the formula to match the specific nutritional requirements of the babies. This was not a good match.

Fraya would now be able to share this newly acquired information with everyone at the seminar. Networking among the many attendees was our way of getting this important information out to all the people who handled raccoons.

The three of us spent the rest of the weekend gathering as much information as our brains could absorb. There was so much to learn. Fraya understood the medical jargon better than Marcia and I did. She had an advantage, being married to a medical student.

When it was time to return home, we were grateful that we'd have the fall and winter to study our manuals before the onslaught of babies ushered in springtime.

There was no turning back now. We promised ourselves that Volunteers For Distressed Wildlife would set the standard for wildlife rehabilitation.

Chapter Six

The Killing Fields

Winter passed without too much wildlife fanfare. Calls were limited to hunting casualties and a few owls needing treatment after having collided with cars. I was busy teaching second grade, playing tennis four nights a week and seeing friends socially on weekends.

Then, in early April, a local farmer who considered the returning migratory birds to be pests in his field of old corn silage, consciously and maliciously planned their demise. He laced rye seed with poison by soaking them together in large barrels. He then spread the tainted seed throughout the rows of shriveled corn stalks. When the flocks of hungry male red-winged blackbirds flew overhead, they were immediately attracted to the seed. Being unusually ravenous from their long journey north, they ate most heartily. Their fate was sealed with the consumption of just two or three seeds. Death would come within hours but not before they suffered from disorientation, loss of body fluids and convulsions.

A neighbor of the farmer became alarmed when she noticed birds dropping out of trees all over her yard. She called Marcia who was on duty as dispatcher that day. This was the first report of trouble though many more calls would follow. Marcia went into action by notifying Ward Stone, pathologist for the New York State Department of Environmental Conservation. He and his assistant were given the location. Marcia also notified an Environmental Conservation officer who joined Ward on the scene.

Ward Stone was acutely aware of the telltale signs of mass bird kills, having been in this line of work for several decades. Whether it be the result of industrial or municipal waste contamination or as in this case, the deliberate act of an individual, the end result always led to his involvement. His mission was to collect specimens for necropsies to determine cause of death and to preserve evidence for future indictments against the alleged lawbreakers. I considered him to be the "Quincy" of the wildlife world.

When Ward and his assistant arrived on the scene, they began looking for the bird carcasses. They found the first victims on property adjacent to the farm. The initial examination made it quite clear that these birds had been poisoned.

After speaking with the farmer and finding the seed spread over portions of the field, Ward contacted Marcia and told her that he needed volunteers to help out. Their job would be two-fold. They would canvas the 140 acres of field and neighboring property, picking up all the dead birds so that other mammals and birds did not eat them and become sick. They would also act as human scarecrows, waving arms and clapping hands to frighten flocks away from the seed.

The farmer was ordered to plow under the Parathion soaked grain but the winter thaw combined with spring rains made his tractor wheels sink deeply into the mud. The seed could not be covered for at least a week.

It seemed like everything was against the birds since only eight volunteers showed up over a two week period. To add insult to injury, the farmer was only fined a thousand dollars for killing over 4,000 grackles, red-winged blackbirds, mourning doves, song sparrows, hawks and meadow larks. He was also banned from using pesticides for the next season. This was considered to be a slap on the hand compared to what fines could have been dealt. It was an affront to us as well because we were aware that there were probably a thousand more dead birds in the killing field that were not collected because of the poor weather conditions which hampered our weeks of searching.

The other farmers in the community took up a collection to help defray the cost of the fine, while we collected the carcasses that were the direct result of his actions. This dichotomy had a profound impact on me. My awareness of man's evil nature was now fortified as the body count increased. Yet this wrongdoing was accepted, even encouraged by some who called themselves keepers of the land.

Marylou had been on the scene almost from the start. I was unable to canvas the property until the weekend because of my job. From what Marylou had encountered, she would need a lot more people to lend a hand.

I picked her up early Saturday morning since she lived only a few miles away from the farm. The weather was unseasonably cold and damp. We dressed in layered clothing and wore high rubber boots. We carried garbage bags to collect the carcasses and carriers in which to keep the sick birds.

The property seemed unnaturally quiet. The occasional gust of wind was the only movement in the adjoining forest. The drab looking corn stalks, left lifeless from winter's harsh treatment, were now the prophetic backdrop for the macabre front and center stage of reality that was suddenly thrust upon us. Our eyes were fixed outward at the endless acres of mud and withered corn. When our eyes shifted to the ground, the evidence of a mass poisoning became alarmingly clear. Dead birds lay at our feet. Their eyes were wide open, their mouths now locked in their final gasp for air. Their legs were stiff and straight.

As our feet and legs began to sink into the mud, we knew that our ordeal would be complicated by our inability to cover the entire 140 acres. With only a few of us each day, we would not be able to canvas the entire farm.

Marylou had become familiar with the property. She noticed some birds that had become sick but had survived were found in the woods to the north of the cornfield. That's where we focused our efforts that day. The mud was not as bad there either so we could walk faster and cover more acres.

It wasn't too long before I found my first struggling victim. It was a beautiful grackle, with its iridescent color shining in the sunlight. It was floundering in a ditch of cold water. I picked it up, unsnapped the top two buttons of my down jacket and put it in between the layers of my clothes. The warmth of my body might keep it alive while I continued to collect more specimens. Each time I found another live bird, I put the one in my jacket into the carrier and put the new, more critical one inside my jacket. Very small birds, like the song sparrows, were kept in my pockets.

I found seven sick birds on Saturday. Sadly, I collected over 500 dead ones. The black plastic garbage bags became so heavy that I had to stop gathering the birds and make the long walk back to our staging area to get another bag. Ward Stone had shown us where to leave the specimens so he could take them back to his lab for analysis. Sometimes he opened the crops on a few of the birds while we were with him, to show us the number of rye seeds that the birds had ingested before they died. No seminar could compare to the lessons learned that day.

My car was parked a considerable distance from the site, because we were not allowed on the farmer's property, including walking his fields. This made it very tiring for me to bring the live birds to the car and make room in the carrier for more pick-ups. Each time the farmer saw us on his land, he threatened to have us arrested for trespassing. We explained to him why we were there, trying diplomatically not to provoke him though we were prepared to be arrested. He walked away disgustedly. Parking on his land further antagonized him.

The bitter cold was now a factor in our own well-being. Our fingers and hands were becoming numb. Depression momentarily slowed us down but our anger would stir us to forge ahead.

Time was also a vital factor in this rescue. If we were to save any more birds, the difference between life and death was only a matter of minutes. The birds' body temperature needed to be raised if they had any chance to be saved. Those that made it home with us were given rehydrating fluids. They were kept warm with heat lamps which they seemed to relish. Food was available to them in their tanks. As they began eating, I was encouraged that they had passed the toxins and probably would make a full recovery.

The second day was much like the first. I didn't look forward to returning but nothing could stop me, either. Marylou and I went together. We parked in our usual place, only to face the farmer's wrath again. Several other volunteers were there so we concentrated our efforts in the woods where we had found the live birds the day before.

When we came back to drop off our filled garbage bags, Ward Stone was there examining carcasses. He opened the stomachs and gullets to show the other people what we had witnessed the previous day. The potency of the laced seed shocked all of us. This farmer's deadly intentions bordered on overkill. The residue alone would be fatal if left in the field uncovered.

My heart was tinged with sorrow as Ward took dove after dove, plucking the feathers to expose the breastbone and crop area. What had these solitary creatures done to this angry farmer to deserve an ending like this? The farmer had claimed that all these birds were ruining his crops. They were a nuisance. Would somebody please explain to me how any birds could be a threat to a year old field of silage?

The next time we went to the farm Marcia came with us. We had kept her informed and she continued to call for more volunteers. She was well aware of the need for more help but the response was disappointing, so she joined the effort. Ralph drove her to a meeting place where we would all go in my car. Marylou and I filled her in on the best way to search the acreage, so once we arrived on the scene we didn't need to waste time planning our strategy.

The three of us walked within shouting distance of each other. Now and then our paths crossed. If we came upon more than two birds, we'd yell for help and come together to catch them and find room for them in whomever's jacket had space.

When we stopped for lunch, we ate in the car with the heater on full blast. We had a little nip of whiskey from a single-serving airline bottle I had tucked away in my glove compartment. It had been served to me on a flight to Bermuda the year before. Since I rarely drink alcohol, I brought it home with me, then forgot until that day that it was in my car. That bottle brought back wonderful memories of a trip that offered such natural beauty. How I wished that I were in Bermuda again instead of this god-forsaken place!

With little time for daydreaming, we returned to the field to pick up another few hundred dead birds. If the farmer's intention had been to kill a specific kind of bird, he had failed miserably, for the dead included hawks as well as songbirds. In fact, we found evidence of body parts of birds outside the entrances of fox dens. Now the chain of affected wildlife was lengthening.

A spring snowstorm soon covered the rye but as soon as the snow melted, a new threat developed. About two weeks after the initial poisoning, the female red-winged blackbirds would return to join their prospective mates. They too would be attracted to the tainted seed. We were called into action again to scare them away. The scene was all too familiar to us now.

We seemed to save more this time. The birds that I brought home were released in two days. They seemed to recuperate faster than their earlier counterparts. Perhaps the wet, heavy snow had diluted the strength of the poison.

I released my seven blackbirds on a pond adjacent to a church that I passed on my way to work every day. It seemed an appropriate place to give them a second chance at life. I could hear them calling, "Conk, conk, kereee," to each other. This would be an ideal place to count their blessings!

This whole experience was truly my initiation into wildlife rescue and rehabilitation. The taste of the struggle, bitter, but the challenge, sweet. I didn't know my own inner strength until I was faced with the plight of these birds. If someone had said to me in my younger years that I would someday be strong enough to face the suffering of animals and not fall apart, I would have thought that to be impossible. Me? That little girl who always cried for Peter Rabbit? That was one of the reasons I had not become a veterinarian. Too sensitive. Too emotional. Well, now there stood a cornfield, simple in its design but oh, so lethal in its plotting.

In between the rows, my epiphany had occurred.

Chapter Seven

Horned Grebes Eating Machines and Hell Divers

It had always seemed as though the animals' comfort took precedence over our own. My dad often joked about meals being served to him **after** the wildlife and our pets were fed.

Certain rooms in the house were systematically being converted into wildlife areas, subtly forcing Dad into relinquishing part of his basement for my wildlife work.

One incident which made us realize that we needed new accommodations was when a horned grebe came into our home. This precious handful was found flapping around in the middle of a highway in sub-zero weather. It was picked up by a passing motorist and left at a local pet store owned by friends of mine. They thought that I would be interested in caring for it, so they kept it in the store until they got in touch with me.

Meanwhile, Marcia and several other rehabers also had taken in grebes that were grounded. They were not injured or sick. Most likely, a storm had blown them off course. None of us had handled grebes before, so that's when our private collection of bird identification books came in handy.

Descriptively known as "hell-divers", horned grebes are fourteen inches long, dusky gray and white with orange eyes and a long neck. They are particularly skillful in the water while at the same time, very clumsy on land. Grebes have feet on which the toe has one or more separate membranes which are connected at the base. The toes are extremely flat while the nails are short and round. The bill is about as long as the head. Because the neck can be extended so quickly, the beak could easily poke out someone's eye. It was important to keep in mind when I handled this bird.

Since it was a particularly harsh winter, with 25° below zero temperatures hitting us for many days, all the waterways were frozen solid. It was assumed that the grebe was grounded by bad weather conditions. Unable to take off from land because its legs were designed for water liftoffs, the bird was totally helpless. What to do for it in the meantime was the sixty-four thousand dollar question!

We began by putting plastic tablecloths on the wall-to-wall carpet in the den. Then I confiscated one of the cats' larger litter boxes. I washed it thoroughly and filled it with water. I was afraid that the city tap water would be highly chlorinated so I purchased a bottle of dechlorination drops and added it to the water. This was repeated each time the water was changed.

I got a large cardboard box from the supermarket, lined it with newspaper and put it next to the "litter pool," for want of a better name. We kept the room as cool as possible by closing the heat vents in the den. We didn't want the grebe to become acclimated to warmer temperatures if its release back into cold weather was only days away. I even made sure that the water in his pool was cold.

The next major problem was finding minnows, since the grebe wanted nothing to do with thawed smelt. The pet shop owner had fed it goldfish, which it loved! I wasn't about to do the same.

The next morning I visited a nearby bait shop. Ice fishing was a popular local sport, so minnows were in stock there. To start, I purchased five dozen fish, hoping that they would last for a few days. At $1.25 a dozen, this was going to be an expensive bird to feed over a long period of time. I asked the shop owner to also save me all the dead minnows. No sense wasting them, since I could throw them into the litter pool along with the live ones. The grebe would be none the wiser.

When I returned home, I put the grebe into the water. In an instant, the master diver used that shallow plastic tray as its own private swimming pool. I started dropping in one fish at a time. Before I realized it, the grebe had consumed four dozen minnows! Not satisfied, it anxiously awaited the next course. It became stunningly clear to me that this horned grebe's voracious appetite would soon deplete my bank account and make the bait shop owner a very rich man.

The last dozen fish were kept for the noon feeding. This was an appetizer, at best. It was back to the bait shop to purchase another five dozen for the remainder of that day and the next morning. I made daily visits to the bait shop, buying seven dozen fish and praying that there would be plenty of dead ones.

The bird only wanted to stay in the water long enough to eat and preen itself. It would then swim furiously around and around, gaining enough speed to jump out. I then put it back into the cardboard box.

I made it a habit to regularly put the grebe in the water. I feared that its feet might dry out and the membranes between the toes might crack. I also noticed that the bird only preened when it was in the water. Preening made the bird waterproof. Dry feathers kept the bird from getting hypothermia. All the more reason to schedule my friend for frequent swims.

I devised a ramp between the box and the litter pool so the grebe could enter the water at will. I used an old rubber door-mat which was waterproof, while at the same time, did not hurt its feet. Everybody laughed at my contraption but it worked. It wasn't long before the bird confidently walked the ramp. Nobody made fun of me after that.

Keeping the water clean was a tough job. The bird's third use for the litter pool was as a toilet. On an average of five times a day, Mom and I carried the water-filled plastic litter pool from the den, down a short hallway to the bathroom. We'd carefully dump the water and rinse out the tray. Mom put the emptied pool back in the den and I followed her carrying pails of fresh water for refills. What a tedious and backbreaking job that became!

Everyone who heard about this unusual bird came to the house to take photographs. When it was feeding time, the expressions on the visitors' faces were priceless. They couldn't believe how much food this handful of a bird consumed. As it dove under the water, it was a matter of two seconds before the fish was caught and swallowed. It was like my money was disappearing down the bird's throat!

I began to supplement the diet with mealworms. The grebe ate them with less enthusiasm than the fish. If I fed the fish to the bird first, the mealworms sank to the bottom of the pool and remained there until I emptied the tray. I had to outsmart this fussy bird by giving it the worms first while hunger was at its peak. As soon as the bird swallowed a few worms, realizing that they were not those delicious minnows, it was useless to try any more tricks. I would give in. When you've got an endearing olympic diver from the wildlife kingdom in your den, you can't help but treat the celebrity like royalty!

Each day I'd pray for a warm spell. The weather reports were discouraging. Old Man Winter was unrelenting that year. While my grebe was doing nicely, other rehabilitators were having problems keeping theirs alive. It seemed ominous that mine was the only one still thriving after seven days. There now was a sense of urgency to get this bird released before signs of stress or illness began to show.

Marcia contacted a conservation officer who was driving to Long Island in a few days. The weather there was milder and there were accessible open bodies of water in which to release the grebe. If I drove to Marcia's and left the bird there, the officer would relay it to Long Island.

Mom and I ventured up the mountain to Berne with our little friend packed comfortably in a cat carrier. I brought enough minnows with me to keep the grebe well fed for several days. Marcia would follow the same feeding schedule as I had, so I brought along the litter pool too.

The driving conditions were rugged, since so much snow had accumulated on the mountain. The slick roads were a challenge as I tried to keep a steady foot on the gas pedal to maintain control while gaining traction. My car was not equipped with four-wheel drive. At times we doubted that we would make it.

The driveway was not plowed. Instead, we could see that the tire tracks from Ralph's truck were the only path to the cabin. After a racing start to clear a snowbank left by a county plow, I took my chances and drove in line with the tire marks. Ralph's truck was much higher than my car. I could feel the undercarriage scraping the snow. I didn't want to have to carry all the supplies in from the road.

All the proper contacts were made to relay the bird to Long Island. I knew the bird was in good hands with Marcia. I set up the pool and water, showing Marcia how eager the bird was to eat. My mind was preoccupied with getting back on the main road and safely returning home. I hated winter driving. If this had been anything else but an animal case, you would not have seen me on the road.

I warmed up the car's engine, slowly pressed down the gas pedal, and off we started. Everything was going smoothly until I found myself hung up on the snow bank at the property's entrance. The snow was at least four feet high. My car was going nowhere. Fortunately, the area was bustling with cross–country skiers, so we waited for some of them to return to their cars which were parked all along the side of the road. We waited about five minutes but no sign of anyone. I attempted to push, then rock the car back and forth but nothing worked. Finally, a skier came out of the woods to lend a hand. He got some old rugs out of the back of his van. He put them under the wheel for traction. We all did some shoveling to clear in front of the bumper. It was time to move that sucker out of there! It worked. There was only an hour's drive left. We thanked the gentleman and started down the mountain.

I hope that the grebe appreciated all the effort that went into its rescue and release. I sure would like to have been there when it jubilantly took flight once more. I can only see it through my mind's eye as the release was related to Marcia when she spoke to the caretaker of the sanctuary. He told her that the grebe dove and swam, preened and ate. It wasn't long before it literally ran across the surface of the water, gaining momentum as it flapped its wings, leading to a glorious flight to freedom.

We now know that the majority of grebes that are rescued in mid winter have developed ice on their beaks and wings, thus causing them to lose the power of flight. Once they hit land, they become stranded and helpless. They can't resume flight unless they are put back into the water. They need a fairly long runway of water in which to take off. If they remain stranded, they will starve, become a predator's next meal or freeze to death. It is only when concerned people get involved that these creatures have any hope of surviving. I was proud to have been a part of that effort.

This experience helped me better cope with the next errant horned grebe who came tumbling to earth one January day in Troy. This time, the bird must have mistaken a blacktop driveway for a patch of water. Having encountered wing icing problems, the force of gravity was too much for the bird to battle, so down it came. As the grebe listed from side to side like a ship on rough seas, the homeowner looked out of her living room window to catch sight of what she thought was a funny looking red-eyed duck. When she called me to see if I could rescue it, her description of this bird could only mean one thing. I was about to have another shot at saving a horned grebe.

When Mom and I arrived at the location, an all too familiar scenario was about to unfold. Sure enough, it was another hell diver. It was not injured, just stranded. We collected this handful of waterfowl and took the male home. We stopped at a bait shop to purchase minnows. We were well aware of what the bird was capable of consuming so we weren't caught short this time. We even had a large kiddie pool on hand in our garage for this very eventuality. He could swim and dive to his heart's content. If the cold spell ended soon enough, we planned to release the bird on the Hudson River, just four blocks from our home.

Weeks went by without a break in the weather. The bird's appetite was forcing us to plunder our emergency fund! We were also concerned about his extended stay in our relatively warm basement. If the grebe stayed too long indoors, the window of opportunity for release would be lost until spring.

About five miles down river, the Ford Motor Company factory had its power plant facility right on the west bank of the Hudson. The power plant building actually jutted out over the river and kept a small section of the river open and ice free. As Mom and I drove around searching for a release site, we spotted this area from the east side of the river. We drove over the Green Island Bridge, which connected the city of Troy to the tiny village of Green Island, where the plant was located.

The plant entrance was heavily secured with high barbed wire fencing and a guard station. In order to get to the river's edge, we would have to obtain permission from the security personnel. How does one explain that there's a horned grebe in my car that needs to be dropped into the river so that he can take off and fly south? Can we have permission to drive onto restricted land to let this poor bird go? Well, that's exactly what I did. As I was explaining myself, the suspicious guard looked as though I was a spy from General Motors. I probably had a video camera in that cat carrier.

"Miss, I'll have to refer you to the Vice President in charge of operations," answered the guard.

I entered the main building and introduced myself to the receptionist. I repeated my story to her. She looked quite strangely at me, paged the Vice President and had me wait in the lobby.

A very distinguished looking white haired gentleman came to the lobby. I introduced myself and told my story for the third time to him. The plight of this bird seemed to touch this executive's heart. He summoned a maintenance worker who escorted us to the shoreline of the power plant.

The three of us drove in my car over icy railroad tracks, past abandoned buildings, getting within 100 feet of the crumbling cement stairs leading to the river's edge. The shoreline that we thought we had seen from the other side of the river was a dangerous precipice. The stairs looked like they were built centuries ago. The maintenance worker offered to take the carrier as close to the water as humanly possible. His safety was in jeopardy as he carefully maneuvered the snowy incline and the broken steps. He opened the box. In an instant the grebe was splashing in the water. We hadn't anticipated the current's force, made greater by the turbines in the power plant. We watched as the grebe seemed to be pulled under water, only to surface for a few seconds down river and then disappear again.

As we stood on the bank, we could feel our hearts pounding through our coats. What had we done? Had we sent our grebe to a watery death? Our eyes scanned the water's surface, hoping for a glimpse of our bird. Sure enough, his head popped up again as he seemed to be pulled underneath the part of the power plant that jutted out over the river. Within a minute, the grebe's head would pop up close to where we were standing. This was some emotional rollercoaster ride for us. We should have remembered that the name "hell diver" comes from their ability to dive underwater for long periods of time. While we mistakenly thought that the bird was drowning, he was having the time of his life!

We stayed long enough to ease our minds. This was play time for our aquatic friend.

No doubt  **about it.**

Chapter Eight

Father Knows Best

T he use of our den for our first grebe was what motivated us to start thinking about separate quarters for the wildlife that would be in our care. Dad offered me a quarter of his basement. One section was his office, another his workshop and the third part was a storage area.

He diligently worked at drawing up plans for the "clinic". It would be 11' by 14' with adjacent living quarters for me, to save me from running up and down a flight of stairs during the hectic spring and summer baby season. I had a sofa bed that I used some nights to stay close to the animals that were critical. Dad had a full kitchen installed, too. It was my own cozy apartment. What was supposed to be a bedroom was used as the "clinic". Eventually the whole apartment was converted into a nursery and clinic. I had an examination area, cages where just mammals were housed and a separate room for birds.

A portion of the backyard was filled with large flight cages. Their design and construction were well planned to ensure the safety and contentment of the birds. Wire was installed under the cage floors so that no animals could dig their way in. Shades were installed all around the cages so that they could be put down each evening to protect the birds from neighborhood cats. Every morning, the shades were drawn to let in the sunshine. The cage floors were covered with clean builder's sand. The sand was sifted every day to clean out the bird droppings. There were wooden nesting boxes inside two of the aviaries. The nestlings could be brought outside in their berry baskets and placed inside the eight-foot-long sections, where they were sheltered from the wind and rain. The enclosures seemed to offer security to the birds when they were introduced to the outdoors. As they became adjusted to their new surroundings, they would hop out of the berry baskets and sit on the ledges of the wooden boxes. When they were ready to take their maiden flights, there were plenty of pine boughs draped across the interior of the aviaries to support their landings. If they missed and landed on the ground, the soft builder's sand would cushion their falls.

The outdoor cages were not built all at once. As funds became available, supplies were purchased. Sometimes neighbors and friends got together on weekends to build my aviaries. In most cases, I hired contractors to do the work. This was expensive, but my cages were models for other rehabers.

Dad, on the other hand, insisted on finishing the job downstairs all at once and he paid for the whole remodeling. He insisted on a generous supply of electrical outlets to accommodate every heating pad and heat lamp that I owned. He had commercial tile installed, knowing full well that there would be a great deal of human and animal traffic on the floors. There were special lights installed in the drop ceiling that simulated sunlight, since the basement windows were not condusive to much sunshine. A full kitchen was built with plenty of cabinet space for my food supplies. A double stainless steel sink was put in for the convenience of washing and rinsing animals. This was the best feature in the kitchen. Many oil soaked birds and flea infested mammals were washed in this double sink.

Dad and I worked side by side with the contractor. I was used to spending lots of time with Dad. He always brought to life my visions of stage scenery that made class plays huge successes. He was a very ingenious man. He could build anything or fix anything. All I had to do was ask and he'd be right there for me. He did everything with a passion, though two major heart attacks would have slowed down any other man.

It took over a month to finish the basement. When everything was in place, the finishing touch was hanging my state and federal permits on the wall. I was ready for business, although no income would be generated from this line of work.

Isn't it strange how the more room we have, the more we seem to need? Each time a great horned owl or a red-tailed hawk was brought to me, I would wish for more cages to house these large birds. I had to hold myself back because our nearly five acres were in the city limits with code restrictions that we didn't want to violate. There was no sense in attracting city inspectors. We had a wonderful working relationship with local law enforcement as well as city representatives. Because our grounds were immaculate and the animals were housed in attractive, secluded cages, our wildlife endeavors were accepted. Besides, I couldn't handle any more than the five outside cages.

On April 11, 1983 my father died suddenly of a massive heart attack. The devastation was so deep for Mom and me that we didn't know how we would go on without him.

The last thing he did for me was to install a brass wood-pecker door knocker that he attached to the downstair's door that led to my apartment. I'll never forget the look on his face when he asked us to come and take a look at the shiny new knocker, perfectly centered on a freshly stained door. Mom had bought it for me the day before on a day trip to Connecticut.

Dad asked, "Well, how do you like it?"

Mom answered, "It's just beautiful, Fred."

"I love it Dad," I added.

Mom said, "The only thing is that it's upside down."

"That's the way it's supposed to be," Dad answered defensively.

"No. Woodpeckers don't eat with their heads pointing down-ward," Mom insisted.

"Sorry Dad, but Mom's right," I said.

Quite admirably, Dad proceeded to unscrew the knocker and put it up the **right** way, though he was not convinced this was the correct position. It was good for another laugh at the dinner table that night.

The next morning he was taken from us. Our world was shattered. The wake and funeral did not stop the wildlife calls from coming in. I did everything to refer the calls elsewhere but for one woman who insisted that she had found a baby pelican on her front stoop. Not even a death in my family could deter her from calling me repeatedly for my help. No matter how much I explained to her that pelicans were not native to Troy, and since she lived only blocks from the Hudson River, she was adamant that this must be a baby pelican. After all, it looked like one!

My Uncle Al saw the frustration on my face. It was only a few hours since we had buried Dad so he offered to pick the bird up, because the woman did not drive. I needed a diversion from all the sadness, so I joined him. I had told the woman to wait on her front stoop for us. I stressed the importance of keeping the bird warm. April was still damp and chilly, especially in the early evening.

Al drove slowly down Fifth Avenue where the row houses line the street. The apartment number was on my side of the car, so I saw the woman sitting on the stairs with two youngsters. We pulled up to the front of the house, expecting to see a box with the bird in it.

"Where's the bird?" I shouted.

"I've got it right here in my bra," she answered. "You told me to keep it warm."

My uncle and I tried to keep straight faces as she plucked a baby **pigeon** from her bosom!

She handed it to me saying, "See. I told you I saved a pelican."

I must admit, the bird was warm as toast.

"Ma'am, this is a baby pigeon, not a pelican," I said.

"Are you sure?" she asked, with a puzzled look on her face.

"Absolutely positive," I retorted.

"I ain't never seen a baby pigeon around here before," she said.

"That's because baby pigeons stay in their nests until they're full grown. You usually only see the young adults at about ten weeks old," I explained. This baby accidentally flipped out of the nest in the eaves of the apartment building. There was no way to return the bird to its home. I was now its foster mother, whether I was in mourning or not.

The four-week-old male raccoon that arrived several weeks after Dad's death jolted us back to our senses with his endless crying. Nothing we tried settled him down. A policeman had rescued him and two others from a fireplace. Choosing to keep two of them to raise himself, he neglected to tell us that our little guy had siblings. But after listening to them screaming for four hours because he had no idea how to bottle feed them, he was at our front door again, eager to pass them on to us.

We had never raised raccoons before, so I called Marylou six times that night. She was our raccoon expert, having raised dozens of them with great success. She recommended a variety of nipple sizes but nothing satisfied the babies' instinct to suckle. I added extra honey to the formula, hoping that the sweetness would encourage them to drink. Finally, after reuniting our male with his siblings and using a preemie nipple that felt comfortable in their mouths, they fell asleep, totally exhausted.

The large sized box that we kept them in was lined with layers of paper. Then three heavy bath towels were placed in the box. A heating pad was positioned under the box for added warmth. They were fed every three hours, round the clock. It took days before they totally accepted the bottle feeding. They were fussy and squirmy, always searching for their mother's warm teats and the security of her heartbeat. Since their eyes were still closed, it was even more heartbreaking to see them groping for their mother. They would whimper, then scream as they felt their way around the box.

All kinds of baby birds and squirrels were keeping us busy. As much as we wanted to comfort the raccoons for longer periods of time, the other animals required our attention as well. The squirrels were easier to feed. We tried to manage their feeding times before we fed the raccoons. The birds were fed every thirty minutes. Before we were even finished feeding the three raccoons, it was time for one of us to stop and feed the birds in the nursery room.

This madhouse deepened our sense of depression and grief. We both felt that things were out of control. We were torn between taking these wildlife calls or taking time for ourselves to come to grips with my father's sudden death. There was the estate to settle, the piles of unopened mail, the day to day chores and my teaching responsibilities. Somehow, we managed to face them all as a team. Just Mom and me.

To make matters worse, the city sewers backed up into our basement. The animals had to be brought upstairs until the water and slime were cleaned up and the rooms disinfected. Then a brush fire nearly burned down the house. It was deliberately set by kids who attended an elementary school just north of us. They had been asked to stay off of our posted property. Their response was to burn the cotton-like seedlings from our tall poplar trees. Two inch thick cotton covered our entire property. These delinquents set fires at each corner of the front lawn. In a matter of seconds, the yard was in flames, fast approaching our home!

A man riding his motorcycle and another in a truck witnessed the fire. They ran to the house and used the hoses that were on reels at the north and south sides of the house. Mom was alone. She tried to call the fire department but for reasons still unknown to us, the phone was dead. She ran to several neighbors' homes for help but most people in the neighborhood were at work. Finally, someone heard her screams and called for help.

I was on my way home from work as the fire equipment arrived on the scene. By then the flames had reached the front sidewalk, which prevented the fire from continuing toward the house. The two men extinguished the flames on the north and south sides of the house. The fire in the back woods was brought under control by the firemen.

Just as the trucks were backing out of my driveway, I was approaching our house which was still surrounded by police and people. The scene frightened me. I thought that something had happened to my mother. She had been under such stress that my mind automatically assumed she had taken ill.

A neighbor ran to my car to tell me that my mother was fine. Nothing else mattered. I pulled out of the driveway to let the firetrucks leave. I briefly surveyed the front lawn from my car as I waited for all the traffic to leave. The cotton from the trees had always been just a nuisance for a week or two before the rain would cause it to disappear into the ground. It was the natural order of things. Sure, it had always made us delay our flower planting tradition for a few weeks. No sense trying to put in our flowers with all that snowy stuff floating around. But this cotton acted like gasoline. As soon as the kids put a match to it, the flames spread over our lawn like fire over an oil spill on the surface of the ocean. Every summer, as the poplars shed their seeds, we are reminded of our brush with disaster. Matches and mean spirited pranksters pushed us to the breaking point.

The animals were none the worse. No matter what had happened outside, the hungry critters inside were demanding to be fed. My job was to assume the wildlife chores when I came home from work, since Mom had taken over for me once I left for school. I had started the day at 5:30 that morning by feeding everyone and cleaning their cages. Then it was time to shower, dress, eat breakfast and leave by 8:15 a.m. Mom held the fort until I returned at 4 o'clock. She then prepared dinner, hoping that I finished my schedule about the same time the meal would be ready. After dinner, which was always interrupted by phone calls from the public, we worked together to feed everyone one last time before getting the next day's formulas mixed and refrigerated. The process would start all over again the next morning.

The school year was full of animal projects. One popular learning tool was the WPET radio network that I created on our building's intercom system. I had a question box outside of my classroom door where any student could drop a note. They could ask any questions pertaining to domestic or wild animals. Once a week, I went on the air to answer their queries. I must admit that their curiosity kept me on my toes. I made it a point to research their well-thought-out questions since they loved to ask the difficult ones.

I was relieved when the summer vacation began. Teaching second grade was my life's work, but all teachers look forward to July and August. My 26 students came to my home for a picnic the Saturday after school closed. It was an annual tradition that made the school year complete. The highlight was to see the animals that they had heard about throughout the year. They were also entertained by a clown while I served them a picnic lunch.

It was a sad day when I left teaching after having injured my back that year while at work. The chronic back pain took its toll. No more tennis or softball or bowling. The wildlife rehabilitation continued in between bouts of bed rest. There were times when I couldn't take another wildlife call. My book does not end here, because with the continued help from my mother and newly trained assistant rehabilitators, our home remained a haven for distressed wildlife.

Nobody's perfect

Chapter Nine

Chimney Swifts

The most memorable wildlife episode was the successful attempt to raise and release chimney swifts.

For several seasons in a row, a lady called to say that there were baby swifts that had fallen into her fireplace. She referred to them as ugly blackbirds whose noise could make the hair on your head stand straight up. I believed her story the first time but year after year, she would bring these birds to me under the same circumstances. The suspicious part was that she brought the entire nest along with the clutch of nestlings. When parent swifts are building their home inside a chimney, you can be assured that the nest is built to withstand any peril. Their salivary glands are well developed and produce a secretion that acts like crazy glue in supporting this mud and twig nest.

My thoughts on the matter were that their hungry screeching annoyed her. Having no patience to wait the approximately three weeks until the birds would begin eating on their own, she made her yearly visit to me. She made no attempt to cap the chimney. It took more effort to extricate these poor birds from her chimney than it would to stop them from building their nest in the first place. She must have taken a long pole, shoved it up through the flue, banged the sides of the chimney until the birds and their nest came tumbling down into her fireplace. How convenient it was for her to just drop the birds at my door, never thinking of them again until the next summer when the adults built a new nest in her uncapped chimney.

You have to understand that swifts and swallows eat while in flight. They are like a vacuum system that sucks in insects by the thousands. They are beneficial to the environment for without them, we could not enjoy the outdoors due to insect overpopulation.

Their eating habits, though helpful to the ecological balance, made my life very miserable because nestling chimney swifts have to be force-fed throughout their time in captivity. The stress that they feel during this period is enough to kill them. Just as difficult was the varied diet that was necessary to keep them alive. Dehydrated, pulverized insect mix did not appeal to them. Even when combined with moist cat food, they fought every mouthful. I resented this woman's selfish attitude. She put me in an unenviable position. I had to come up with a better way to care for these unique birds.

As with all the other mammals and birds that came to our facility, I did research on their habits and needs. The swifts were fascinating to study. With every page that I read, I was more and more convinced that they were going to be my challenge for the season.

Young swifts are naked when hatched. For several weeks they are fed in the nest. After that, they leave the nest and cling to the wall beside it. The vertical surface of the chimney's interior poses no problem to swifts. Their short legs and odd looking feet, though totally unfit for perching on branches, do ever so nicely clinging to rough surfaces. Their short tail feathers are spiked with tiny needle-like protrusions, adapted to give the birds additional support. Since they can't perch, they spend most of their time in flight.

Their black feathers and dark eyes, combined with their ability to cling to walls like bats, sometimes lead people to misidentify them as they effortlessly fly through the air in swooping patterns to catch insects.

As far as the swifts were concerned, a brick was placed in a fishtank instead of the usual berry basket. The three semi-feathered nestlings clung to the surface immediately. Side-by-side, heads peering over the top edge of the brick, they watched my every movement.

My mealworm farms were producing healthy, juicy specimens. I used them as the exclusive protein diet because of my previous dismal attempts to use unappetizing mixtures. I also fed them grapes for moisture.

When I walked into the nursery, the swifts began squealing for food. The minute I approached their beaks with the mealworm and tweezers, they would close their mouths and cower. Once I gently forced open each beak, a cavern-like throat was exposed, offering a peek into the world of this avian marvel.

Each baby ate about six worms every half hour. I fed them from left to right and then from right to left, thinking perhaps I could pick out one that was less stressed than the others. Since they moved around the brick like musical chairs, maybe the varied feeding direction would help both the birds and me.

At first, I did not look forward to feeding them. I was so afraid I would injure them. Try to imagine my left hand supporting the bird's back, neck and head while my right hand was gently prying open the beak to force-feed it.

I could tell that they were all not the same age though the difference in size and feather development was hardly noticeable. I guessed that they were born within one day of each other, making the first one three days older than the last one hatched.

As each day passed, my hopes for their survival increased. It was not uncommon to have birds die suddenly, even after they seemed to be doing very well. I couldn't let myself fall into a false sense of security. Only time would tell.

On the fourth day the oldest swift began accepting food without being forced. A simple quick tap on the beak with my tweezers was all that was needed to open that once clenched beak. My excitement was short lived when the other two younger birds were less cooperative. I was grateful for that much of an improvement. At least there was hope that the others might learn from the leader.

The next two days brought added relief as the second and third nestlings started to readily accept food. As they matured, they adjusted to this method of hand feeding. Now, anxiety free, I faced each feeding with renewed enthusiasm. The birds showed no sign of stress. Their chance of survival was steadily improving. I considered their piercing screams as music to my ears. Those same sounds were what caused the homeowner to repeatedly vacate them from the premises. Isn't it interesting how we each view our world in shades of acceptance? One saw the birds as pests, while the other saw them as blessings.

Before long they were transferred to our outside aviary, still clinging to their brick. I placed them in one of the wooden nesting boxes that was attached to a center wall that separated two aviaries. The front of the box was left open so the swifts could fly out whenever they were ready to fledge. Now they would be called fledglings. The brick was steadied against another larger patio brick, from which they loved to hang.

There were all kinds of song birds in this sixteen foot aviary, including a barn swallow, a wren, thrushes, doves, house sparrows and a fresh little house finch named "Zazoo."

Zazoo had to check out these new residents. She flew right into their box and introduced herself as queen of the Ziter avian kingdom. The enlightened swifts made no attempt to question her authority.

All the songbirds lived peacefully together except for the starlings, who were usually aggressive toward their cagemates. I found it necessary to have another aviary built exclusively for them. The swifts and all the other youngsters lived in serene quarters, just eating and growing and learning all the outside sounds that would help them to adjust to that harsh world that was only weeks away.

The chimney swifts grew stronger with each passing day. They loved being outdoors. They began exercising their wings at about the fourth week. When I would go to the cages to feed everyone, I'd find them attached to the cage hardware. They flew right back to their brick when they saw me open the container of mealworms. It reminded me of the times I enjoyed as a child, visiting farms where the cows automatically came back to the barn at milking time. All these swifts needed was to see me open the cage door. To them, I was the milk of life.

Staunch animal lovers like myself are often criticized by those who favor the scientific approach for what they perceive as projecting our emotions onto our animals. Some say that it's absurd to think that birds and mammals are capable of displaying human characteristics such as gratitude and affection. Take it from me, they are wrong. It is arrogant to think that humans hold the exclusive rights to exhibiting emotions, leaving the animal kingdom to react just by instinct. My chimney swifts taught me that.

When it was time to release the swifts, I wanted to find a spot where other swifts were more abundant. The only place where they were seen was several blocks from my home, down by the banks of the Hudson River. Unfortunately, a large supermarket/drugstore complex and a fast food restaurant made that spot unfavorable for their release. I felt that the site would be confusing and dangerous for the birds. There would be too much pedestrian and vehicle traffic.

The safest choice was in my own backyard. If they weren't ready for the freedom, they could be recaptured and put back into the aviary. If they were ready to be on their own, at least they would have each other for both protection and company. Chances were that they would join a flock soon after their adjustment to this big new world.

Mom and I waited until early evening. We put the three birds on the trunk of a tall poplar tree, where they could climb to the top and then take flight. A book that I had read had recommended using a telephone pole for this staging area, but the pole was too close to the road. The tree was not far from their aviary if they chose to return home.

The two older swifts took flight almost immediately. My heart was pounding with excitement. They circled the backyard several times, flew to our neighbor's brick garage and attached themselves to the wall, resting for only a moment before flying off beyond our view. The youngest one never left the poplar tree. It never even moved. We wondered if perhaps the three day difference in age made it that much less prepared for independence. Rather than leave it vulnerable to the cats in the neighborhood, I brought it back to the aviary for the night. The message was clear. The bird was not ready to go yet. I was saddened that now this lone swift would be separated from its siblings. If only I had been gifted with the power of prophesy.

The next morning there was no sign of the two released swifts. I was busy as usual, cleaning cages, feeding twenty-five hungry birds and twelve squirrels. Five o'clock that evening, the single swift appeared restless. It flew around the aviary in circular motions. All day long it showed no desire to fly. As I stepped out of the aviary, I heard the familiar sound of swifts. As I looked up, a flock of more than sixty swifts began circling the house and aviary. They were flying lower than normal, skirting the roof of our ranch style home. Where they had come from was a mystery to me. I had never identified swifts on the property before, but soon realized that they were the same birds that in past years had flown overhead every night. The difference was that they were like tiny dark dots in the sky, flirting with the clouds. Now they were putting on an aerial display for my benefit not more than ten feet from my head! I was able to pick out my two swifts from this flock because they flew closer to me with each passing swoop. They were also smaller than the others.

The sky was now filled with vocal swifts. The noise brought my mother out to see what the commotion was all about. Then, the lone swift called to the other two. I opened the cage door, allowing the bird to join its siblings. They all circled the aviary, passing me close enough to touch my cheeks with their wings. Never once did I worry that they would hurt me. Around and around they flew, coming down to gently make contact with my hair.

As if this was not startling enough, they began to land on the front of my blouse. With those dark eyes peering up at me, my heart melted. They had come to use my blouse as a feeding station, clinging to the material with confidence and enjoying my company. I used to let them stay there as I fed all the other birds. It was something that they were accustomed to doing ever since force-feeding was no longer an issue. I think that they looked forward to this bonding time as much as I had. Now they were attaching themselves to my blouse for only a minute or two, flying back to the flock to resume eating. Sometimes only two landed on me. When one would leave, another would take its place.

Mom stood by me hoping to receive their favor. She was rewarded with the same display of affection. We could not hold back our tears. The experience was so overwhelming that the very hand of God had seemed to touch our faces with each passing stroke of their wings.

"Hi, babies. Come on, babies," I called to them. They would only join the flock to eat again and then return to us.

As nightfall approached, the flock disappeared, but the youngest one remained on my blouse so I decided to put the loner back in the cage on the brick. It was only then that we regained our composure, returning to the house to sit down and talk about what had just taken place. It was like a vivid dream. Who would believe such a story? I couldn't wait to call Marylou and Marcia. Repeating the events to them excited us all over again. We needed to calm down long enough to resume our chores.

We could speak of nothing else that night. Let the biologists or scientists give their explanations. I say that it was a gesture of love. A parting "thank you" for all that we had done. What we didn't realize was that this display of gratitude was not over.

We waited for their return the next evening. The caged swift's uneasiness that I had noticed the day before was now showing again. Would we be lucky enough to be revisited by these wonders? Yes. It was the second coming of the flock!

Flying ever so low, they circled us at rooftop level. Then, upon release of the youngest swift, came our other two, ushering their sibling up to the hungry flock. Once again the trio ate heartily from the sky's banquet table, leaving every so often to land on our blouses. Playfully, they flew at our heads, almost daring us to duck.

"Oh, please don't stop," I pleaded. Somehow I knew that this experience would never happen again in my lifetime. I wanted more and more. My soul felt like it was being lifted to the heavens along with my birds.

That second night saw the youngest swift join the flock. I was pleased that it had not been left behind. I had mixed emotions about never seeing my birds again now that they were all together. Maybe the only reason the swifts had returned was to just rescue the one in the aviary.

The third day seemed to drag as we anxiously awaited another encounter. The birds really had no incentive to come back unless they still had some attachment to us. Like clockwork they returned. Our three were flying stronger and more confident of their style and grace. They touched our faces and landed on our clothes but only for a few seconds at a time. The rest of the flock maintained their flight patterns, keeping watch over their new family members. It was apparent that our birds were equally influenced by their need to be with us and their strong instinct to be with the flock. When they were on our blouses, their eyes would shift from our faces to the flock and back again. The pull toward the flock was palpable as their feet clenched the material while their wings fluttered to fly away. Mom and I talked to them, encouraging them to join the flock. Clients have often asked me how I can part with these creatures after becoming so attached. It is the true nature of love to accept what is best for these birds and all my wildlife. Captivity is not the right choice for them.

The third night was just as thrilling as the other nights. We were blessed with another reunion. It was like watching the constellations and trying to pick out our favorite stars. The sky was full of swifts. It was becoming more difficult to identify our three birds but we had come to accept this as a good sign. They had made a wonderful adjustment.

By the week's end the flock was flying at its normal altitude, much higher and less well defined. We were learning to come back down to earth ourselves. There was much work to be done. We had taken in three times more than we had released so we had to concentrate on the animals still under our wings.

It was impossible not to look upward each time we were in the yard. The sky held a special moment in time that clouds could not cover nor the rain wash away. We had done everything to save them.

They had given us so much more!

Chapter Ten

Premature Gray Squirrels

Gray squirrels are common in the northeast. People don't pay much attention to them unless they are trying to outsmart them at their birdfeeders. They consider them to be backyard outlaws. Every conceivable device has been marketed to stop or at least discourage the squirrels from getting to the birdseed. Nothing that I've ever tried prevented my squirrels from getting to the sunflower seed. Their teeth chewed through plastic, wood and metal. Their acrobatic talents made my obstacles a mere detour! Why was it necessary to keep food from them anyway? Their survival was just as much a struggle to them as it was for the birds.

I built a tray feeding table with a roof for protection against rain and snow. It was four feet long, allowing birds and squirrels enough space to eat together. The rest of the yard had regular bird feeders. As my observations helped me to better understand the animals on the sanctuary, I decided to attach five gallon buckets to six of the large trees and fill them with sunflower seeds. The squirrels could sit inside of them and eat to their hearts' content. This made the other birdfeeders less of a target for the squirrels.

I also noticed that the eating habits of birds differed depending on the specie. Some birds, like the bluejays and pigeons, would knock seed out of the feeders onto the ground where juncos, starlings and doves would be waiting to feast on the leftovers.

The feeders were of particular interest to me because I had released so many squirrels and songbirds on the property. It was fun to try and identify the wildlife that I had raised.

A special pair of gray squirrels that were always recalled with great fondness were lovingly named "Mr. Munchkin" and "Mr. Chubs". They were born prematurely in early March. They were found in an attic nest after their mother was killed by a telephone installation man. I presumed that she was protecting her litter of newborns from this intruder. She lunged for the man as he climbed his ladder to begin the job of installing a telephone line. The female squirrel was killed before the man realized that she had just given birth to two tiny, pink and hairless babies. The attic was the perfect place for her nest until the telephone man disturbed it.

The owner of the house took the two squirrels from their nest, called a neighbor, who then called me. I was not prepared for squirrels so early in the season. The warm spell in mid-February probably had brought about an early mating season. I had hoped to be carefree for just a little longer but one phone call changed all that.

I made arrangements to meet the woman at a halfway point because she was not willing to drive the forty-five minutes to my house. I knew that if those babies had any chance for survival, I needed to get them right away.

I brought a hot water bottle in a cardboard box with a towel warmed up in my clothes dryer. A fish tank was prepared with a heating pad and placed by my bedside. I knew that constant monitoring of their condition would be necessary. This meant checking their body temperatures, hydration level and feeding schedules both during the day and throughout the night.

I asked my cousin Marina to go with me. Our original plans to go shopping together were set aside to save the squirrels. Changing plans midstream became a fact of life once I became a rehabilitator, and this was no exception. Marina willingly came along to keep me company.

After a long wait, a car pulled up to the driver's side of my car. Then a woman got out, approached us without any box or carrier which would have been a clue that she was the person delivering the squirrels. Marina and I looked at each other as she came to my window. She put her hand in her jacket pocket and took out a small square of flannel material with two tiny creatures curled up inside.

"This was the only way I could think of to keep them warm," she explained.

"My God, they're tiny," I said as she handed them to me.

I opened up my box and gingerly placed them as close to the hot water bottle as I could. They were lively and very hungry. It had been more than seven hours since they became orphans.

Both squirrels were five centimeters long. The umbilical cords were fresh. Even more disturbing was the fact that their internal organs were visible through the skin. The eyes were not fully developed. Their bodies were truly embryo-like. It was imperative to get them home as soon as possible. We stayed there only long enough to explain to the woman how critical these squirrels were. The two of them in my hand barely filled my palm. When I closed my hand I felt their heartbeats and knew that I was in for the mother of all challenges!

As is the case with every new rescue, I felt the surge of adrenaline through my body as I drove home. My mind was going over every detail of what had to be done once we arrived.

My mother anxiously awaited our return. She had made sure that the heating pad in the fish tank was turned down to the low setting after she had left it on high for about a half hour. The formula had been prepared before I left so it was just a matter of warming up the small amount needed to feed them. I estimated that because they were so small, an eyedropper full would be more than enough. They drank six drops each.

After their first feeding, their tummies felt taut. They needed to be stimulated to relieve their bladder and bowels. This was necessary after every feeding until their eyes opened in about three weeks. Until then, I fed them every two hours with a narrow plastic pipette. A standard eye dropper was too thick for their mouths. I sensed that their delicate bodies would need special handling. It was good that I had set up their tank right beside my bed. I could hear them crying when they were hungry during the night. Response time would be faster.

I must admit that after three weeks of the day and night feedings, I was totally exhausted. If they had not been so critical from the start, the night feedings would not have been necessary. To be awakened twice during the night made it nearly impossible for me to sleep soundly. I seemed to be in an altered state of sleep, always anticipating their cries for food. Once they had been fed, it was not easy to fall back to sleep. Why bother? In two hours time I found myself rolling out of bed again to warm another formula. After that, it wasn't long before the alarm went off, heralding another full day of wildlife and personal responsibilities.

Three days after arriving, the squirrels' skin became dry and scaly due to the proximity of their dry heating pad. I purchased a moist heating pad. There was a sponge-like insert that could be dampened and placed inside the cover of the pad.

At the same time, one of the squirrels, (Mr. Chubs) began crying after each feeding. It appeared to be colic. He would quiet down when I held him but the minute I placed him on the towel, he began to squirm around and cry. His bowels were normal and his appetite was excellent. His condition puzzled me. Mr. Munchkin seemed fine. The daytime feedings did not seem to cause the degree of discomfort to Chubs as did the evening feedings. The little squirrel's distress was as predictable as the sunset. My lack of sleep, compounded by the anticipation of Chub's nightly colic attacks, made life miserable for both of us. In desperation, I put warm water in a measuring cup, submerging the little guy up to his neck in the cup. Almost immediately he eliminated gas. He was fine until the next feeding. If I had been overfeeding him, then why didn't Munchkins have the same symptoms? I had no answers. I drove myself crazy trying to find the cause. I tried Gatorade, then goat's milk, then Isomil. Finally, after ten days, my last resort was to stop stimulating them after each feeding. My theory was that gas pockets formed when the bladder and bowel were emptied and the formula was entering the digestive track too fast. This seemed to be the answer because Chubs improved dramatically.

The next hurdle was to prevent infection and loss of toes due to the skin condition that developed earlier. I contacted my local veterinarian, describing the cracked and reddened skin, as well as the raw looking toes. He recommended Silvadene cream applied to the toes three times a day. I must emphasize that their toes were extremely tiny. The moist heating pad had prevented any further skin irritation but where scabs had formed around the toe joints, circulation was cut off, causing some toes to blacken and die. Just looking at the toes was traumatic for me.

I placed them on antibiotics to ward off an infection that could kill them. My main concern was that they would have enough toes to climb trees and handle food. I suffered more emotionally than they did physically. In fact, they seemed to thrive.

The toe stumps healed nicely after ten days of treatment. The squirrels were now sleeping throughout the night, while their daytime feedings were three hours apart. Munchkins and

Chubs would not be by themselves any longer. Other orphan squirrels were brought to us. Although they were too small to share a tank with the new arrivals, I had planned to introduce them to their fellow playmates in the coming weeks.

A vacation that Mom and I had planned six months before was just two weeks away. Marylou and Marcia had both offered to care for our wildlife patients. Since Marylou lived closer to a veterinarian and had a driver's license, it was decided that she would have the unenviable task of being foster mother to Chubs and Munchkins. Both women had shared my day-to-day worries. They had given suggestions when I needed second and third opinions.

The last thing Marylou wanted was to have my squirrels develop complications and die while they were in her care. I didn't like placing such a burden on her shoulders, but Mom and I really needed this vacation since it coincided with the anniversary of my father's death. We could not bear to be in the house where he died. The objective was to get away for that week.

I brought the squirrels to Marylou the day before we were to leave for South Carolina. I included all the essentials: formula, cereal, medications, bedding and fish tank. I had kept a detailed log of their progress. Marylou continued the diary.

No sooner had we headed south, when Munchkins stopped eating. Acting listless and near death, Marylou rushed him to the veterinarian. He diagnosed his condition as pneumonia. Lincocin was prescribed but the doctor did not give Marylou much hope. She was devastated by the prognosis. She had visions of my returning from the trip only to find out that one of my precious squirrels had died. She did everything humanly possible to save Mr. Munchkins and she was rewarded with his complete recovery.

By the time our trip was over, both squirrels were healthy, growing babies. Marylou was more than happy to return them to me. As I read her diary, I really appreciated her efforts to save my squirrels.

At four weeks old, the squirrels were introduced to Cheerios, walnuts, pecans, grapes and apples. The crumbs from the Cheerios filled their towel. There were slivers of nuts found all over the tank. They wasted more than they ate, but it was all part of growing up. They were learning about their strong teeth and hoarding their food under their towel. I also gave them cherry tree twigs with fresh buds to savor. The squirrels had no trouble handling their food. The missing toes did not limit them in any way.

As their fur grew thicker each day, the heating pad inside the tank was removed and placed underneath. I gave them a small cardboard nesting box which was filled with paper towels. That left little room for them to play so I transferred them and their box into a cage. What fun they had hanging and climbing the wire. It seemed like a palace compared to the confines of the tank. Again, their two missing toes posed no handicap to these capable youngsters.

When the time came to introduce Mr. Munchkins and Mr. Chubs to the other squirrels, I picked a litter of five who were approximately the same age. It was an important phase for them. If they were to gain their sense of wildness, this would be the first step in accomplishing that goal. The litter had been much less handled by us. They were healthy orphans from the start who required less contact with us. This made them play more with their siblings and less interested in humans.

I was a bit apprehensive at first because I was worried that Chubs and Munchkins would find their littermates too aggressive. How wrong I was! Within twenty minutes, they were all playing and roughhousing as if they had been raised together from birth. Within an hour, they were all curled up in their box, sound asleep. Despite their earlier medical problems, Chubs and Munchkins were tough little rascals who showed no signs of weakness or fear.

Over the next few weeks, observing the litter interacting was a priority. Their sleeping, eating and grooming habits were all the same. The only clue that I had been their foster parent was that they would jump on me whenever I opened the cage to clean their living quarters. To them, my body was a race course. Up and down my torso they went in a circular motion. Then they jumped back and forth from the cage to my body as if it were their own private jungle gym set. Catching them to put them back in the cage was a new take on the old "cat and mouse" game!

The next step was to transfer them to a much larger cage. When they were acclimated to that one, the cage was taken outside for several hours a day. The sunshine and fresh air seemed to energize them even more. Soon it was time for their introduction to life totally outdoors in a cage designed and built for mammals.

The big day came when they were three months old. I opened the cage door to let them have their freedom. It didn't take them long to venture into the woods that bordered our property. This cherished land was theirs to enjoy during the daylight hours. At dusk, they all returned to their nesting box in the cage. That was the nice part about being able to release them on our sanctuary. It would be a gradual release, less stressful for both human and animal. Within a week, they had literally carved out a new home by enlarging the hole in one of the wooden nesting boxes that volunteers had built and placed in trees throughout our woods.

My job ended with a great sense of pride. The experience taught me more than any book or lecture ever could. There is no substitute for common sense or sacrifice. Wildlife rehabilitation should not be a hobby. There's too much at stake. Although I would not want to repeat the events of the last three months, I wouldn't trade them for the world.

Chapter Eleven

"Please Don't Keep Me Hanging"

I had made it a policy not to raise or keep pigeons. This came about due to many years of accepting sick ones that carried contagious diseases. It was too much of a risk to expose all the songbirds in the nursery to the viruses common to pigeons.

Whenever nestling pigeons were brought to me, their care included tube feeding. This reinforced the imprinting instinct. I was now their life-long mother. They never left the property. At night they expected to return to their cages through the windows in the basement. Even if I released them miles away, the birds found their way home, usually before I did!

My new plan was to refer pigeon calls to people who raised them. Over the years I had rehabilitated many domestic racing pigeons that had been too exhausted to finish the race. Some suffered fractured wings and legs. I could identify the owners through the leg bands on each bird. A telephone call to local association members became routine. I had made some connections that I'd hoped would assist me when the pigeons came my way.

If there was no one available to help, I set fractures and sent the pigeons home with the clients. Two weeks later I examined the birds again, recommending when the birds could be released.

Baby pigeons were another problem because they had no fear of people. The ones that I released on my property loved to greet clients by flying on their heads. I cringed with fear as the startled victims' response was to flail their arms, trying desperately to knock the birds out of the air, away from their faces. All I needed was to have a heart attack victim sprawled across my front sidewalk, a casualty of the paranoia generation that watched too many showings of the Alfred Hitchcock movie, "The Birds!"

While I was able to objectively rationalize my decision to stop accepting pigeons, my new set of rules was overpowered by my subjective soft heart. Sue Bennett, a longtime friend, was staying with us the week before Christmas. Sue and Mom were home while I was out running errands. The telephone rang. When Mom answered, a hysterical woman with a high pitched voice spoke.

"Is Denise Ziter there?" she asked.

"I'm sorry, she's not home at the moment. This is her mother. May I help you?" Mom answered.

The woman said, "My daughters found an injured pigeon on the bridge by our home. It's in pretty bad condition. The kids are very upset and we need Denise's help."

Mom said, "We usually don't take pigeons."

The lady cried, "Oh, please help us. The children are absolutely hysterical over this bird. Couldn't you please help us?"

"I can't make that decision. Denise is the rehabilitator but she's not here right now," Mom replied. Sobbing could be heard in the background. No matter what their mother said to console them, the girls insisted that only the "bird lady" could save this poor pigeon.

Mom sympathetically said, "The best I can do right now is take your name and number. When Denise returns, I'll have her call you."

The woman begged, "Oh, please make sure she calls me back. Please don't keep me hanging!"

When I did return, about twenty minutes later, my mother repeated the whole conversation. I recognized the sense of urgency that the woman was exhibiting. It was so typical of the myriad of emotions and frustrations that people feel when dealing with wildlife emergencies. I wasted no time in calling her back.

"Hello!" a shrill voice answered.

"Hello Ma'am. This is Denise Ziter, wildlife rehabilitator. I understand that you called about a pigeon," I said.

"Oh, thank God you called. I'm at my wits end here. The girls won't stop crying. The pigeon seems worse!" she exclaimed. Now I could hear screaming in the background.

"It's dead! It's dead!" the daughters cried.

"Denise, you've got to take a look at this bird or else my girls will go off the deep end," the woman insisted.

"All right. Put the pigeon in a small box, but first put an old towel in the box so that the bird can cling to the material for support."

"We'll be there in ten minutes. Whatever you do, don't give the girls any bad news, if you know what I mean," she warned in a lowered voice.

"Don't worry. I'll do everything I can to save their bird," I promised.

Sue and Mom were curious to see how I handled the situation. The mother and daughters appeared more distressed than the bird, or so it seemed. From the tone of the mother's voice and the excessive anxiety in the children's behavior, my psychological savvy was about to be put to the test. My years of being a second grade teacher would come in handy. Diplomacy and nurturing were my strong points. I would need them to get me through this day!

When they arrived, I brought them downstairs to the clinic. They were very relieved when they saw all the cages and tanks situated on three long tables. They gazed at the framed wildlife photographs on the walls. These were displayed to show the many wildlife patients that we had treated over the years. They were somewhat distracted, which gave me a moment to take the box and begin to examine the pigeon.

I slowly opened the shoe box, trying not to startle the bird. As I lifted the cover, I could see that the bird was on its side, legs straight out and eyes wide open. I put my hand inside to pick up the patient. As I touched it, my suspicion that the bird was dead became convincingly clear. The poor pigeon's body was stiff as a board! Rigor mortis had set in well before the bird ever got to my house. In fact, it would not have surprised me if the pigeon was dead on the bridge where the girls had discovered it! I had all I could do to keep my composure. God forgive me but this thing would have made a terrific paperweight!

I knew that the mother wanted to spare her daughters, so when the older sister asked me if the bird was going to be okay, I did what anyone in my position would have done: I lied!

"Is it badly hurt?" asked the worried youngster.

"It doesn't seem to be in any pain, honey," I answered as I put the cover back on the box.

"See Michele. I told you it would be in good hands with Denise," the mother said with confidence.

"What do you think happened to it?" asked Michele.

I said, "It might have flown into a car or maybe someone poisoned it. I'll keep it for a few days. I'll examine the bird **after** you leave because the bird must be very frightened with all four of us standing over it."

I gingerly ushered them out of the room. The girls wanted to pet their pigeon one last time but I told them that wild birds don't like to be touched. (Dead birds don't care.)

Michele asked if she could call back in an hour to see how the bird was progressing. I handed her my business card with the phone number on it as I escorted them upstairs.

"Girls, didn't I tell you that the bird wasn't dead?" said the woman, as they walked to their car. "It had its eyes open."

I waved good-bye, shut the door and ran through the house shouting, "It's deader than a doornail!"

Mom, Sue and I lost our composure. Whatever semblance of professionalism I had demonstrated, not five minutes before, had totally disintegrated. I still felt that cold, hard body against my fingertips, as I repeated the whole episode to them. They agreed that I had done the right thing. Now the problem was how to handle the call from the little girl.

As the three of us sat down to dinner, once again delayed by wildlife priorities, the phone rang. We looked at each other with wide-eyed anticipation. At that point the I.R.S. would have been a more welcomed caller!

"Hello," I said.

"This is Michele. I'm the girl who brought you a pigeon about an hour ago. How's it doing?"

"It's resting very nicely," I answered, truthfully.

Michele continued, "We want to bring you some seed tomorrow on our way to school. Could we see the pigeon then?"

"Oh, uh, I won't be here in the morning," I stuttered. "I teach second grade".

"When do you think you'll let it go?" she asked.

I said, "There are lots of pigeons here so I'll release it right on my property. There are so many pigeons that it will be impossible for you to pick yours out."

"Oh, thank you very much," Michele said.

Her mother then got on the phone. She asked me if I remembered her from years ago when we bowled together. The conversation lasted over fifteen minutes while our dinner was getting cold for the second time. I was relieved that the bird was never mentioned in that part of the conversation, only to be put on the hot seat again, just as I was ready to end our chat.

"The bird wasn't dead was it?" she asked.

I hesitated. Then, through muffled giggling, I answered, "It's fine."

Sometimes we must treat the emotional needs of our clients as well as the physical needs of the animals. This wildlife rehab work is certainly not one-dimensional. I feel like a psychologist, a veterinarian, a nurse, a teacher, a naturalist, a diplomat, a fund raiser, a dog catcher and a farmer all rolled up into one person who is expected to be this super-human being. I didn't think that I had signed up for such a job description, but there was no turning back now. The title of "Volunteer Wildlife Rehabilitator" on my license just doesn't do it justice.

Now it was time to try my third attempt at dinner. The excitement of this work always made me less relaxed at meals. Sue and Mom were already enjoying their dessert. With the next wildlife call only minutes away, there would be no dessert for this "bird lady."

Chapter Twelve

The Power of Positive Stinking

It took me many years before I had enough courage to handle baby skunks. I tried to limit my rehabilitation work to birds but it wasn't in my nature to turn away any distressed animal. I often found that I would accept mammals and then chide myself for not sticking to my original intention of specializing in birds. They required the most care because baby birds must be fed every half hour. Not too many people were prepared to commit themselves to this much work.

The baby skunks raised by Marcia were precious. Much like kittens, I could not help but find them appealing. The only hint of their capacity to spray came from a harmless musky odor that was noticeable on their soiled towels which were changed regularly. My time with Marcia had helped me to appreciate their benign nature.

Each skunk's marking was different. The white stripes running down the back were unique in design and length. Some stripes were wide while others were narrow. This made it easy to recognize each baby, especially if the litter was large.

Once I became accustomed to holding and feeding the babies, my apprehension of getting sprayed seemed to lessen, though I still had a very healthy respect for the adults! I was just glad that I could leave them in Berne. Marcia had hutches where the adolescent skunks were housed, far from the cabin in case something or someone was to spook them.

The day came when I was asked to transport a skunk to Berne. Even though it had been hand raised by Marylou, I was not as confident as she was that her skunk would appreciate my chauffeur service. However, Marylou had helped me out on several occasions so it was my turn to return the favor. This striped wonder would have the **smoothest ride** possible.

I used my father's full size car because I was also transporting seventeen quail to Berne. Mom had offered to keep me company. Little did she think that she would be holding a skunk in her lap! She was somewhat protected by the nice cozy box that housed the skunk for the trip. The towel inside the box and the small holes on the top and sides of the box helped to muffle the sounds that might alarm the skunk's defense system. We prayed for light traffic, no fast stops, no sirens or horns and no potholes. One wrong move and it would be trade-in time on the family sedan!

All went well despite our fears. Mom found herself carrying on a continuous conversation with a skunk whom she barely knew. Maybe her soft voice had a calming effect on this pampered passenger. I was convinced that it made **me** feel better as I skillfully maneuvered the winding roads up the mountain.

The following year, it was my turn to act as foster mother to several baby skunks. The agreement was that I would only have them on a temporary basis, until I could get them to Marcia. The people who rescued the skunks lived in my area, and they were not willing to drive all the way to Berne. This predicament left me no alternative. I did not want them to die. With encouragement from Marcia, who had not been sprayed by any of her skunks during the 22 years that she had rehabilitated, I accepted these baby skunks into my home.

Each day that passed brought me closer to being more at ease with them. Before long, I looked forward to their feeding time because I could play with them, as if they were domestic kittens. Never raising my voice, and avoiding rough treatment, guaranteed me spray-free encounters. By the time I was ready to transfer them to Marcia, I was more confident that I could probably handle another litter in the future. It would be a long time before the call came. Meanwhile I was perfectly content with my birds, squirrels and occasional opossum.

The real test of my dedication arose from a telephone call from the New York State Police. The dispatcher relayed information to me that had just been radioed in to their headquarters. A dead adult female skunk was found on the side of a country road with two youngsters still by her side. It appeared that they were not completely weaned, though they were a good size. Several passing motorists called the troopers' station to get help for the orphans. Since no trooper in uniform was about to rescue them, I was contacted to attempt a rescue. My name and number are on file with all the area police agencies so my reputation as a wildlife trouble shooter was about to be tested once again. However this time, the **trouble** and the **shooter** happened to be the skunk!

Against my better judgement, I told the dispatcher that I would drive to the scene and take a look. Unwilling to leave me to my own devices, Mom came along as my faithful sidekick. Having fallen into the trap of thinking that our volunteer work had ended at a reasonable hour of the day, we had to change from our pajamas back into our clothes. We then gathered up our supplies: long leather gloves, a carrier, two nets, a flashlight and the directions to the spot where we'd find the wildlife casualties.

As our mission of mercy was about to begin, a friend was driving by our house and spotted my car as I was backing it out of the garage. I looked in my rearview mirror to see a car pulling up in the driveway, the driver literally blocking me from getting out of the garage. I did not recognize the two occupants of the car, because it was getting dark. Then I realized they were my friends, Sandy and Eloy Rivage, who had been out to dinner with Sandy's mother who lived up the road from us. As they were returning home, Eloy spotted my car and decided to tease me by causing gridlock in my own driveway. No time like the present to recruit volunteers for our mission! Mom and I coaxed Sandy to join the expedition. She was dressed meticulously in a white pantsuit with matching accessories. Not exactly the wardrobe for a skunk rescue. She probably planned on being the rescue crew's casual observer. We could depend on her for moral support and a few good laughs!

With Eloy following us just long enough to get himself home, the three musketeers continued the trek to the Pinewoods Avenue Extension. Sandy waved to her husband through the back window of the car. She was probably trying to figure out how a relaxed evening of dinner with her husband and mother had spiraled into being whisked away in the back seat of the Ziter's car to some mosquito-infested area to save skunks.

We laughed and chatted all the way to our destination. Then it was time to settle down as we concentrated on locating the skunks. I drove at a snail's pace with my emergency flashers blinking in the darkness. The car's high beam lights were our only source of illumination on this deserted stretch of country road. We strained our eyes to catch a glimpse of the dead female. Her body was on a spot in the road where it was dangerous for us to park. The curve in the road just beyond us made our rescue very dangerous. The sloping ditch, then thick brush, really made it easy for the two youngsters to run away whenever they felt threatened.

The dead skunk's body was bloated and stiff, yet the two young skunks stayed right by her side. It was difficult to distinguish them from the female. The minute they saw the car pull up, they ran into the ditch and through the thick brush. The thought of those frightened babies being left there to suffer the same fate as their mother spurred us into action, even though we were all concerned about getting sprayed.

I parked the car beyond where the skunks were huddled. Mom watched for on-coming cars while Sandy and I got the equipment. Heavy gloves were our only protection. I walked very slowly toward the orphans. One ran down the embankment out of sight. The other baby stayed with its dead parent. Sandy held a cardboard carrier open, waiting for me to capture the poor animal. I approached the skunk with the careful movements of a bomb squad expert! Sandy stood in front of the skunk and I stood behind it. I was able to pick up the fully furred baby and place it in the box. That seemed too good to be true. Sandy closed the carrier and gave a sigh of relief.

We surveyed the area with our flashlights, hoping to spot the other baby. The mosquitoes were eating us alive. We went back to the car to escape their attacks. Before long, the second skunk returned to its mother's side. I crossed the road to make my second rescue attempt. The minute it saw me, down the embankment and into the woods it ran. This happened a dozen more times. It was a waiting game. Mom and Sandy waited in the car and I waited in the bushes! I became the designated animal catcher by default. After all, I was the licensed wildlife rehabilitator. I chose this avocation. The other two were just along for the ride.

Sandy and Mom remained in the car for the next hour. They called out to me every so often to make sure that the "lady in waiting" was alright. The animal was not cooperative. Every time I came close, the skunk disappeared into the night. Back into hiding I went to await the next meeting. The dead mother's body was the magnet that drew this creature back to the road's edge. Once in a while, a car passed us slowly to watch as I made my unsuccessful capture attempts. The lights of the cars always sent the skunk into a panic.

The waiting time seemed endless. The only choice I had was to get the extension handle net from the car and try one last time. I positioned myself close to the female, well hidden by the brush. If all went well, the net would be long enough to drop over the skunk when the time was right. Finally, out came the orphan, down came the net. I caught the skunk but I also made an instant enemy! Mom and Sandy brought the carrier over to me. As I placed my hands over the net to pick up the skunk, I was sprayed! The penetrating odor nauseated me. I don't know how I managed to get the skunk into the carrier with its sibling. I wanted to die! I had taken the gloves off earlier because they were clumsy. Now my hands, arms and upper body were victimized by an ungrateful skunk.

When we got to the car, the odor coming from the carrier spread through the car's interior. My cohorts and I didn't know whether to laugh or cry. Doing anything too loudly further jeopardized our already horrendous situation. As we tried to collect our composure, a couple drove up to my side of the car.

"What happened to the skunk babies that were here?" they inquired.

Before I could answer, the smell from my car permeated the air. There was no need to explain.

"What are you going to do about that awful smell in your car?" they asked.

Disgustedly I said, "Sell the darn thing!"

"What will you do with the skunks?" the man asked.

"They'll be released as soon as they are eating on their own," I promised.

The couple wasted no time in driving away from the offensive smelling car. We did not have that option. Taking the source of the odor with us was the only way that our mission would be a total success. It was the longest fifteen minute ride that we had ever endured. We used the time to come up with a plan of action to rid myself of the smell. Everything I touched in the car was affected. I was teased all the way to Sandy's house. As she left the car, she wished me well. She also had the nerve to say that she really enjoyed herself! Well, I've always been known to provide a few good laughs now and then. This night was no exception.

Once home, Mom searched the pantry for all the tomato juice and canned tomatoes. I put the skunks and their carrier in the empty side of one of my aviaries. I gave them plenty of food and water. It was now eleven o'clock, but it would be four more hours before my head touched the pillow. I wanted to crawl out of my skin to escape this olfactory torture. After throwing away every stitch of clothing, including my shoes, I began scrubbing myself with tomato juice. Two hours of this cleansing made my skin burn from the acidic nature of the tomatoes.

When I finally went to bed the smell still lingered on my hands. The pillows even smelled like skunk. The nerve endings beneath my skin were inflamed. The itchy, burning sensation kept me awake most of the night.

The car wasn't too bad the next day as I prepared to drive the skunks to Marcia's. They were good passengers all the way. That made up for their poor behavior the night before.

Marcia was expecting me that morning. She had been raising five baby skunks who were now old enough to be housed in an outside hutch, a distance from the cabin. They were about the same size as my two. Our plan was to introduce them to the litter by placing mine in the exercise area of the hutch while the litter was in the nesting box. One at a time, a skunk came out to investigate the new kids on the block. We stayed in the background, talking very calmly to the group. They were accepted without any problems. The past twenty-four hours had taught me a lesson in humility. I wore my badge of courage for many days thereafter but the sight of those two happy babies, playing with their new family, was incentive enough to face another day and another challenge.

Two months later, the seven skunks took one last ride. Their release site was on a 150 acre farm owned by friends of mine, Ted and Mary Film. They didn't mind skunks at all. I often used this beautiful land to give my wildlife a second chance.

Chapter Thirteen

Anything But Wildlife

As if I didn't have enough work to do with the wildlife, I found myself raising a litter of five orphaned kittens, a domestic rabbit, a puppy, an exotic cockatoo and a rooster! The only redeeming factor was that they were not all under my roof at the same time.

The three week old kittens came from the grandmother of one of my students, Julie Winters. The mother cat had wandered off and gotten hit by a car, leaving the owner with five helpless kittens, not yet weaned or litter trained.

I guess my reputation as the teacher who loved animals prompted Julie to approach me in the classroom with her request to save the kittens. My whole class knew about the predicament and anxiously waited to see how I responded.

The kittens were not accepting the formula that Julie's grandmother had purchased from her veterinarian. They had not urinated in two days either. They were so young that their mother was still stimulating them after each feeding so it was necessary for the foster parent to take a warm cloth and wipe the private area of each kitten to make sure they eliminated waste. Otherwise, the kittens would die of uremic poisoning. For this reason, I told Julie that she could bring the kittens to me. Besides, to turn down such a plea would blemish my reputation in the eyes of my students. A teacher has an obligation to be a good example to her pupils.

When Julie got home from school, she called her grandmother to give her the good news. That evening, Julie and her mother brought the kittens to my home. I had prepared bedding, warmed by a heating pad placed under a box. I raised them much like my other orphaned babies except that I had the luxury of playing with them much more frequently than my wild babies since they were domestic pets.

The little fur balls relished the warmth. After their bodies regained the proper temperature, I fed them with a pet nurser bottle. They were hungry enough to accept the nipple without much fussing. Stimulating them was no problem either.

The kittens were with us for a month. As the weeks went by, the wildlife calls increased dramatically. All of my fish tanks and cages were now occupied. Our attention had to be directed to the latest arrivals. Our friends loved to drop in to play with the kittens, and we welcomed their help. On more than one occasion, I questioned my own sanity, but Mom was right there to assist me. As much as we loved the kittens, we were relieved when it was time to return them to their owner. When we heard that they were all adopted, another chapter of our life's work had come to a happy conclusion.

Mom and I promised each other that we would not burden ourselves with domestic animals again. It was too much to handle in an already hectic household. Then came a phone call from another student of mine, Gregory Lewis. He and his family were going on vacation for a week. They owned a pet rabbit. Gregory asked if I would babysit his rabbit, "Megan". They would drop off the rabbit the night before they were to leave. All I had to do was keep it in a cage with food and water. They convinced me that very little work would be required. How could I help one student and not the other? Given the circumstances, I gave in and said I'd take the rabbit for the week.

When they brought Megan, I was stunned by the rabbit's enormous size. I did not have a cage big enough to allow her room for exercise. I cordoned off a section of the clinic floor instead of confining her to a cage too small for her comfort. That was a bad decision. The next morning there were rabbit scats all over the place and urine so deep, not even the triple thick newspapers lining the floor were enough to soak up the mess. This was not the intent for which the clinic had been built. Thank goodness my father had had the industrial tiles installed when he designed the clinic. Out came the mop and disinfectant. The rabbit would have to be satisfied in a large cardboard box that I got from the market. Though it seemed like a boring life for Megan, I had no choice. I made it a point to let the rabbit out to roam the clinic while I was downstairs. I kept an eye on her whereabouts. This appeared to be a safer alternative.

Along with the discovery that rabbits are not litter trained, I also learned the hard way that they also love to chew. While playing with Megan one afternoon, the doorbell rang. Instead of putting her back in her box, I left her unsupervised in the clinic while I answered the door. My unexpected visitors stayed for several hours. That gave the rabbit plenty of time to chew through the telephone line, then on to the lamp cord, followed by an extension cord for dessert! She also ignored the newspapers that were on the floor for her benefit. I don't understand how she wasn't electrocuted. My faith in guardian angels was bolstered that day. It was my only explanation for why these exposed wires did not cause a fire.

Time to sanitize the clinic floor again. The rabbit was confined to the box for the remainder of the week. All the wires were replaced by an electrician. We paid dearly for my stupidity, but things could have been much worse.

My new resolution was to politely refuse to take on any more domestic animal requests. Time has a way of healing all wounds and also dulls our memories enough to let down our defenses. A year after the bunny episode, a very caring, sweet college student called me about some robins who had fallen from their nest, situated on a second story ledge of her dormitory building. There was no way to return the nestlings to the ledge so I told her to bring them to me. We took an instant liking to each other. Lisa was from Florida. She was preparing for final exams, just before spring recess. She showed a great interest in my work, staying for hours to ask questions and watch me feed the animals.

I heard from her again when she called to inquire about the birds' progress. Shortly after that, she called to ask whether I knew of a pet adoption agency that might locate a home for an abandoned puppy. She had saved it after witnessing the dog's collision with a hit and run driver. After having taken the pup to an animal clinic for treatment, she placed an ad in the newspaper, hoping to reunite the dog with his owner. No one claimed him. She put up posters around campus. The owners were never found. Lisa had grown attached to the dog. She was now faced with the decision to keep the sad eyed mixed breed or put it up for adoption. That's where I entered the picture.

I sensed that a strong bond had developed between dog and rescuer. Lisa had not only tended to the dog's wounds, but she brought the timid, shaking pet from a bundle of nerves to a happy, well adjusted pooch. She really wanted to keep the dog.

Her dilemma was that she was going home to Florida for semester break. Who would take care of her dog while she was away from campus? Like a magnet that attracts the weight of the world; like an obsessive gambler who knows she should not put her last dollar on a long shot; like a spectator at an auction who scratches her nose, only to end up with a monstrosity, I offered to dog sit!

I kept "Adair" downstairs but since he was only several months old, I found it necessary to take him for frequent walks. This was another animal who was not housebroken. I borrowed a long chain to be able to leave him outside for short periods in the afternoon. He managed to dig craters whenever he was tied. Our perfectly groomed backyard fell victim to his bad habits.

When he was alone in the cellar, my office furniture became the focal point of his nasty chewing habit. Anything that wasn't nailed down became his toy. What happened to the shy, timid puppy that Lisa had described to me?

His three week stay proved that dogs are even more destructive than rabbits. Lisa was mortified at the damage caused by Adair. She made a donation to my organization. I was left with the cost of furniture restoration. I have not seen or heard from her since, but I suspect that she enrolled her dog in some type of obedience training classes.

If you think that resolutions are made to be broken, you are absolutely right. A call in December from our Troy Police got me involved in "The Case of the Wandering Cockatoo." Found strolling down Fifth Avenue in the city, the bird was picked up by a concerned citizen who took it to the police station. The dispatcher called me to ask if I would take it until the owner was located. I was entertaining guests at the time, but I agreed to help out.

A reporter from *The Troy Record* newspaper was monitoring the comings and goings at the station that day. He had a photo taken of the bird as it sat on the Desk Sergeant's hat. The reporter sensed that a good human interest story was about to unfold, so he recorded the bird's destination in order to contact me later that night for an update. The cockatoo was brought to me in a police patrol car, not unlike the many times before that the police had come to my door. My guests thought that this was a novel way to be entertained. My friends were becoming accustomed to our phone calls somehow changing our ordinary days into newsmaking stories. There was never a dull moment in the Ziter household.

The white feathered Australian Parrot looked dirty and weak. Its primary feathers had been clipped so it was unable to fly. The police had fed it peanuts, which it devoured. The bird was given the royal treatment at the station, and now was escorted in the cruiser with continued regal attention.

I transferred the bird to a large cage with various size wooden perches. I filled dishes with sunflower seed, pieces of oranges, apples and nuts. As a precaution, I put an antibiotic in the water because the bird had been exposed to very frigid weather that cold December day. This exotic creature was not adapted to biting cold temperatures and snow. Pneumonia was a strong possibility.

The bird made the front page of the Sunday morning edition. Our telephone never stopped ringing. You wouldn't believe how many people claimed ownership of this expensive bird. I realized that I was in for a good bit of detective work to separate the con artists from the legitimate owner.

It was encouraging to receive calls from people interested in giving the cockatoo a good home if the owner could not be found. I made a list of their names and numbers, promising to get back to them in a few days. *The Troy Record* printed daily updates of the bird's condition. It was like a soap opera of the animal world. This publicity even prompted a woman to call me and ask if I would sit for her macaw while she went away for the Christmas holidays. I declined.

When I was satisfied that I had located the bird's real owner, their reunion took place after a four-day stay with me. The owner said that her pet had been missing for three nights. She had given the bird a misting with a portable shower head in her bathtub. She believed that the bird escaped from the cage soon after the bath. Her children, who were running in out of the house, left the back door open, and out walked the cockatoo. More amazing was the fact that the bird walked down two flights of stairs, crossed many streets, wandered more than eight blocks before arriving in downtown Troy.

When the bird was discovered missing, the woman did not think that it could survive the cold. She even doubted that the celebrity bird featured in the paper might be hers. How did her pet ever make it to Fifth Avenue? No harm in calling just to see if the leg band on my cockatoo matched the numbers associated with her bird. Miracle of miracles, they were identical! To further prove that this was her bird, the woman said that she had a bill of sale for her pet. She also was able to describe a hardly noticeable peach colored patch under the bird's neck. I raised the feathers under the neck and there stood the patch. This was her bird.

The bird was named "Fortune" because that was how much it had cost. The bird had only lived at that residence for seven months, having been purchased in a private sale. Birds do not like changes in their lives. It's sad to think that they are passed from household to household over the span of their long life expectancy. Could it be that this bird was trying to return to a former owner? We will never know. I think that "Misfortune" might be a more appropriate name.

As many times as I had promised myself that I must stand firm and not accept any more pet problems, I found it impossible to abide by my own decision. Case in point involved a newborn puppy found in a gutter. Now how could I ignore the plight of this animal?

A telephone caller explained to me that her son was walking to the corner store for a quart of milk. He noticed something move in the gutter. Out of curiosity, he approached the curb to get a closer look. Peering down, he heard what he thought was the whimpering of a puppy. The body was so small and wet that its birth must have just taken place. There were no other puppies around and no female either. He decided to take the puppy to his apartment and call his mother for some advice. She then called me.

I explained that I was a wildlife specialist. I don't know why I bothered to tell her this because it never seemed to work on any other callers. She was familiar with my work, having read about me in the newspapers. She offered to pay for a taxi to pick up her son and deliver him and the puppy to me. Against my better judgement, I relented. I had no alternative since animal shelters are not equipped to raise newborn puppies.

Within twenty-five minutes a taxi pulled into the driveway. Although the son did not have directions to my home, the taxi driver, once given my name, knew exactly where I lived. He had read many articles about me too. Little did he know that his animal delivery service was about to prosper!

The puppy was wrapped in a towel. When I peeked inside, I saw a flat faced black animal with eyes sealed shut and umbilical cord still fresh. I had no idea what breed or mixture the puppy might be. The birth sack covered the body. The mother must have been frightened off as soon as she gave birth. Usually, the female cleans all the pups. The little one fit perfectly in the palm of my hand. I couldn't help but be reminded of the preemie squirrels that I had raised many years before. I prayed that this tiny puppy would suffer none of the complications that the squirrels had endured.

I washed the male pup in warm water to remove the birth sack. He started to whimper. Being hungry was a good sign. I heated a special puppy formula called Espilac. He was a cooperative eater. As with all baby mammals, I stimulated him and then placed him on a towel warmed by a heating pad. A ten gallon fish tank was more than adequate for his size. His fur had not grown in yet. Keeping a constant temperature in the tank was managed with a thermometer.

I contacted the Troy Animal Control Officer to have her patrol the vicinity where the pup was found. I suspected that there might be more puppies in trouble. None turned up until eight weeks later, when two puppies who were said to have been found in a large grocery bag were picked up by the Troy Animal Control Officer. They looked exactly like my pup. We surmised that the owner of the female allowed her dog to roam the neighborhood. She must have had the first puppy in the ditch, then run home to give birth to the rest of the litter. When the puppies were weaned, the owner probably didn't want them any longer. She made up a story about finding them in a shopping bag and called the Dog Warden to take the dogs off her hands. This was a common practice to trick the authorities into picking up unwanted pets. When the Dog Warden saw these two Shepard pups, she was convinced that they were the sisters of my orphan.

We named our puppy Cody. He was the perfect patient. The feeding schedule was every two hours, gradually extending to three and then four hours. Cody outgrew the fishtank in a matter of weeks, graduating to a playpen that was loaned to us. Without the enclosure, he loved to terrorize our cats. It was also a terrific housebreaking tool.

It was difficult to part with him after ten weeks in our care but he was going to be a large mixed shepherd who would certainly frighten the animals in our outside cages. It was time to place an ad in the paper to find a good home for this lucky dog. We received many inquiries. Mom and I interviewed all the potential owners and agreed on a young couple who seemed to bond with Cody on their first visit. We insisted that the couple pay two more visits to make sure that this dog was ideally suited to their needs.

When the adoption day came, the new owners made an appointment to have the veterinarian give Cody his first series of shots. We sent them home with all the toys that Cody had come to love. We filled a box with his favorite dog food and treats. In return, they promised to send us photos. For a year the pictures kept us up-to-date on the dog's growth. At fifty pounds, his great appetite made him into a healthy, muscular canine. Adding to our joy was the happy news that Cody's sisters were both adopted. One went to Marcia Kent, while the other was given a wonderful home with the Animal Control Officer who had saved her.

A taxi wasn't the only mode of transportation that delivered animals to our doorstep. An ambulance driver brought us an injured bird. Even more impressive was the sight of a stretch limousine pulling into our driveway to drop off another injured bird. The chauffeur opened the door of the limo, assisted four young women out of the car and escorted them to my front door. They handed me a small box with a bird inside that one of the girls had rescued earlier that morning. The girls rented the limo for the day to take them to Lake George, but not before getting help for their feathered friend.

Firemen are on twenty-four hour shifts. This made it impossible for them to bring me a nestling bluejay that fell down into the fire station's living quarters in Cohoes. They were unable to leave their posts and I was alone at the house, unable to leave the clinic. They chipped in enough money to hire a taxi to bring the jay to me. Remember the driver who brought the puppy to my place? Here he was again, about to hand me a box large enough to hold a television set! It must have taken up the entire back seat of the cab. What were those guys thinking? Bigger is not necessarily better! I was impressed with their determination to get the bird to me without delay. I only hope that the cab driver was told what was inside the box. Otherwise, his imagination might have led him to believe that he was transporting a dalmatian from the firehouse to the Ziter house!

Many injured and orphaned wild animals were brought to us by law enforcement officers. It was not unusual to see a State Trooper, Sheriff, Conservation Officer or Troy Police vehicle parked in our driveway. I often wondered what our neighbors thought when they saw the police at our door so regularly.

Despite the many official vehicles that were used to transport wildlife to our clinic, the limousine seemed the most original. Then came the mobile veterinary van, fully equipped to make house calls. The sight of this converted recreational vehicle parked in our driveway was the talk of the neighborhood. It was like an emergency room on wheels. It was a luxury to have the animals treated right at home, when the vet was in the area.

I wish that there had been a doctor on hand when a rooster needing medical attention was brought to me. The story begins one Saturday night about 8 o'clock. The rooster was found running down a city street behind four teenagers on their bikes.

While cruising along, one boy turned around to see a rooster trailing behind him. He shouted to his friends to come back and help him catch this neat looking bird. The foursome chased the squawking bird into a backyard, cornering it by a fence. They captured it and brought it home. Since one of the boys had made it a habit to collect and observe reptiles and other species of wildlife, his mother was not surprised to see her son and his cohorts proudly showing off their latest find. Fearing that the bird might become a permanent resident, the young man's mother called the police.

When the policemen arrived, they found the rooster confined to a milk crate in the middle of the caller's living room. The boys were reluctant to give up their new pet but they had no choice in the matter. The rooster was transported to the police station where a reporter and photographer were waiting to interview the two police officers as they booked their latest "jailbird".

After all the excitement had died down, the big question was what to do with the bird? The Animal Control Warden was not on duty, so the rooster would have to be kept in the "Property Room" or maybe Denise Ziter, Wildlife Rehabilitator, would be willing to take him temporarily.

Officers Joslin and Mahoney dropped the bird off at my house after the Desk Sergeant called to ask for my help. The bird was in very poor condition. The crest atop the rooster's head and several of his toes were missing. The natural spurs on his legs were gone. It was clear that wounds around the ankles were the result of leather straps drawn tightly to hold the substitute metal spurs used in cock fights. Thankfully, he had fought his last battle in the pits of hell. His nights of abuse at the hands of evil people who enjoyed this blood sport were over. His enemy now was the threat of infection.

I administered antibiotics, made him comfortable with a heat lamp and cleaned his wounds. My heart ached for this abused animal. The cruelty had not diminished this bird's gentle nature. As I tended to the many fresh abrasions, I took notice of all the old scars. It hurt to imagine what this bird had been through before he somehow escaped his tormenters.

At the police station the officers had fed the rooster raw rice, which he ate without hesitation. Though their intentions were good, uncooked rice might kill the bird when he drank water, causing the rice to expand in the bird's stomach. There was nothing I could do but wait and see if he lived through the night. I wasn't overly optimistic. There were too many years of mistreatment, too little time to heal. I convinced myself that his death would be peaceful here with us.

At 5:30 the next morning, we were awakened by the "cock a doodle doing" of Mr. Rooster! My 15 year old Pomeranian, who slept in bed with me and who we thought was totally deaf, sat up. Her ears perked as she listened to the rooster's call. Mom came into my room with the biggest smile on her face. We then ran downstairs to confirm with our eyes what our ears couldn't deny. The rooster continued his serenade as we giggled in delight.

I wanted to have a lasting remembrance of that morning, so I set up my tape recorder. Mr. Rooster cooperated fully. Later, after the sun came up, I called the police to let them hear the rooster in all his glory.

After recuperating with us for several weeks, I was confident that the rooster was in the best condition of his life. Despite missing a few toes and his natural spurs, his cuts had healed completely, his appetite was extraordinary, and the antibiotic therapy had cleared up any infections that were lurking in his system. What a difference in the appearance of his feathers too. The shafts were showing new growth and his preening improved the damage done to his existing primary feathers.

His recovery did not go unnoticed. The rooster acquired celebrity status when his picture and story appeared in yet another Sunday edition of *The Troy Record* newspaper. Although we received many calls to inquire about his recuperation, I still needed to find the perfect home where this once battered bird could live out the rest of his life in peace, without the threat of literally fighting for his survival. The perfect place was with Marcia's barnyard menagerie. Dexter, as he was lovingly named, was soon the happy protector of nine hens who lived in a barn with a sheep and a goat, both formerly abused pets. If the animals could talk, oh the stories that these dusty old walls could hold and the creaky old floors could tell. A simple barn, fresh straw in their stalls, freely offered food were now symbols of their deliverance from man's cruelty.

The "girls" accepted Dexter. His meek and gentle nature was a welcomed change from the previous rooster who terrorized the barnyard. Visitors to the Kent's cabin were greeted by this beautiful and proud bird as he freely pecked at the grit in the driveway. Not all humans were his enemy.

We had taught him that.

Chapter Fourteen

Momma Opossum
&
The Seven Dwarfs

We've had wildlife brought to us from as far as one hundred miles. It always amazed me that clients were willing to drive many extra miles to bring the animals to us. We served a five-county area. There were many other licensed rehabers living closer to them, but few who specialized in birds. It would have been nice to limit myself to the avian world, but too many mammals needed my help as well.

In contrast to the many miles traveled was the mother opossum who was critically injured as she tried to cross New Turnpike Road, directly in front of our home. Mom witnessed her plight as she looked out her bedroom window, to see a truck driver pushing something off to the side of the road with a stick. The man then returned to his vehicle and drove away.

Mom suspected that an animal was hurt, so she gathered a box and towel that we always kept handy in the garage. Off to the road's edge she went. As she approached the injured opossum, the animal began to crawl toward the center of the road. She was dragging her fractured hind leg, determined to save two of her babies that were still in the middle of the road. There were seven babies in her pouch at the time of the collision, but these two were thrown out on impact. Wearing long gloves, Mom rescued the family. She brought them downstairs to the clinic, making them comfortable until I came home. I was busy making my weekly visits to retailers who donated supplies and food to Volunteers For Distressed Wildlife. The opossum definitely needed veterinary care. Mom made the arrangements with the staff of the Lansingburgh Veterinary Hospital, just around the corner from our home.

I no sooner entered the house when Mom described the eight new cases downstairs awaiting my attention. The babies were not injured but were only four inches long, not yet weaned. Their mother's condition was tenuous. She not only had an apparent leg fracture, but her tongue was severely lacerated and swollen. Cuts and bruises covered her body. Her injuries did not stop her from hissing as she stood in a posturing position to defend the babies who were hanging from the coarse hair that lined her back. I spoke softly to her as I slowly put my hands in the box to remove the babies. It was not necessary to bring the babies to the veterinary hospital. I anticipated that X-rays would need to be taken. Momma opossum might need to be sedated or if she had internal injuries, I might not be bringing her back home. In either case, it was best to separate them now.

Mom heated up some formula to feed the seven pouch dwellers as I prepared to take their mother to the veterinary hospital. With so many other animals to feed, Mom had to take over the daily routine while I took on this emergency. These unexpected trips seemed to drain me of what little energy I had in reserve. The ever-present sense of urgency coupled with the possibility that I might be expected to make a life or death decision, always placed added pressure on an already stressful lifestyle.

The X-ray showed a compound fracture of the tibia. The sedated opossum needed anesthesia in order to tolerate the pain associated with the application of the cast. The leg was so badly broken that we were not sure the cast would work. I was sure of one thing. This groggy mother was not in any position to nurse her babies for at least forty-eight hours. The drugs administered to her for sedation now contaminated her milk. Mom and I were now the official surrogate parents.

Once back home, Momma opossum was placed in a box next to her brood. She slept soundly most of the night. The youngsters were not happy being away from her. When she started coming out of the anesthesia early the next morning, she frantically climbed the sides of the box to reach the babies. I picked up the babies to let her see and smell them. If they stayed outside her pouch, they would not nurse. Her milk was still toxic to them until the next night. Her tongue was cut so badly that she was not able to eat. Thank goodness I was trained to administer liquids and nutrients by IV drips.

The cast was bulky. Still dazed by the trauma, the opossum used every ounce of energy to keep track of her babies. She became upset when they were taken from her to be fed or when I needed to treat her wounds. This was going to be a long recuperation. The cast was to be changed in four weeks, followed by another x-ray and a new cast. Then it would be another three weeks before the removal of the second cast.

When the babies were reunited with their mother on the third day, she was strong enough to nurse them and they were anxious to return to her pouch. It seemed to us that they had grown in just the three days that we had fed them. Hard to imagine that they started out the size of bumble bees. Not fully developed, these embryos attach themselves to her teats as they use her pouch as an incubator. As our only marsupial, the opossum should be looked upon with fascination rather than disgust. If you were to see the way this mother overcame her disability and pain to care for her seven babies, I'm sure your opinion of her as an unattractive over-sized rat might change.

If female and babies had to stay with us for several months, I insisted that they be given the biggest enclosure that we could fit in the clinic. I started calling appliance stores to ask for a refrigerator box. When one was located, a friend with a truck delivered it to me. I put the six foot long box in the hallway leading to the clinic. I placed it horizontally so that one of the sides was now the top. I cut the top out. This made it possible to see all the activity that was going on inside. I covered its floor with layers of paper. A carrier was put on one side of their new domicile so that the family could have some privacy.

Mother and children found the accommodations to their liking. They investigated every inch of the box. The food was placed in the opposite corner from where they slept. It wouldn't be long before the youngsters were trying solid foods. They loved cheese, meat, mixed fruit yogurt, grapes and even thawed mice which we had on hand for our birds of prey.

The refrigerator box was somewhat of an occupational hazard for me. Every time I leaned over the box to replace the soiled papers or change the food, the edge of the cardboard cut into my waistline. Yikes! I had black and blue marks that resembled a set of train tracks around my midriff. I met my quota of bend and stretch exercises every day and I had the bruises to prove it!

It was now time to have a new x-ray taken. We would find out if the weeks of care were worth the effort. It would be horrible if the bone did not heal. Our attachment to Momma opossum was painfully sentimental. She had been such a wonderful mother. I was not ready to consider anything else but a good prognosis. My prayers were answered. The x-ray results were encouraging. A new cast and three more weeks of confinement in the refrigerator box just about guaranteed her chances of release back to the wild.

The Troy Record newspaper published her story too. She and her babies were very photogenic. Momma was like the poster child for unappreciated and underrated wild mammals. The cast on her hind leg touched the hearts of all who read the article. Carrying her babies on her back added to her new image.

This otherwise patient mother had reached her limit after ten weeks in captivity. Her cast had been removed several weeks before. Her healthy, strong offspring had become an annoyance to her. It was time to set them free. Having scouted out many locations, I decided on the farm of Mary and Ted Film. There was a shed on the property that sat on an embankment so a good portion of the foundation was open. It seemed a perfect starter home for the family.

The ride to Buskirk was filled with great anticipation. The release site offered Momma and her young 150 acres to explore, should they choose not to live under the shed. As soon as I opened their carrier, Momma waited to see what direction the babies were headed and she ran in the opposite direction! Ten weeks in a refrigerator box with the seven dwarfs was enough for her. The song, "Don't Fence Me In" came to mind as we scanned the woods to catch sight of the opossums. Their speedy retreat proved that opossums are not always slow moving creatures.

Another myth  **bites the dust.**

Chapter Fifteen

Don't Call Us, We'll Call You

The publicity generated from my wildlife work was making me well known. This celebrity brought far more animals to my doorstep than I ever thought possible. I never dreamed that each year, hundreds of distressed animals would need my help. Very few people were available to deal with the unique problems of wildlife care, making my services even more demanding.

During the busy season, usually April through September, the ringing of the telephone dramatically increased. I found it necessary to carry a portable telephone with me into the aviary while I fed the birds and tended to the cages. There seemed to be no respite from that ringing device!

Sometimes the the public called me in the middle of the night as if I ran a 24 hour hotline. I didn't think the calls were funny at the time, but my recollection of them now sheds light on the humorous side of these conversations.

One February evening, about 10 o'clock, a gentlemen called asking for the lady who took care of wild animals.

"That's me," I answered.

"I've got something here that I think you'd be interested in. It's what ya call it, uh uh . . . a caterpillar," he said.

"Oh," I answered.

"It's black in the front, black in the back and brown in the middle," he described.

"That sounds like a Woolly Bear Caterpillar," I said.

He couldn't figure out why the caterpillar was in his driveway in the middle of winter.

I said, "Probably this mild break in the weather, combined with the thaw, made the caterpillar escape the mud and retreat to the safety of the paved driveway."

"Yeah, well are you interested in taking it?" he asked.

"I don't know that much about insects," I replied.

He added, "I had it on my kitchen table for awhile and it was straight out."

"What do you mean by that?" I asked.

"You know. Like a number one. But then when I put it on my radiator it curled up like a zero!

"My God, get it off the radiator!" I yelled.

I gave him Marcia's number and told him to give her a call. She would be able to tell him what to do to save it, if indeed that's what he wanted. Perhaps she knew someone whose forté was entomology.

I chuckled to myself, imagining the conversation that must have taken place when this concerned gentleman called my unsuspecting friend. I expected Marcia to call me momentarily to give me a hard time for referring such a call to her. Instead, the man called me back to fill me in on how to become a foster parent to a Woolly Bear.

He had been instructed to put the caterpillar in a glass jar with a stick for it to climb. He was to place a tiny bottle cap with water in the jar and drop some lettuce in for food. It was vital to put small holes in the jar's lid to allow oxygen to enter.

The kindhearted man thought he would share that information with me, in case I should ever get a call like his again. I thanked him for his concern.

Each new episode seemed to top the ones before it. The telephone calls were no exception. An old three-story factory building was being gutted to prepare for renovation work and eventual use as an apartment complex for senior citizens.

Over the years, several families of barn owls had nested in the building's upper floors and tower. As the construction crews began their work, the owls were disturbed. Being nocturnal creatures, their sleeping time was disrupted, causing the birds to leave the structure during the daylight hours.

One owl was spotted in a backyard of a near-by house. The owner of the house was very upset because neighborhood children were throwing stones at the frightened bird. It seemed confused and disoriented. The heartless children were unrelenting in their efforts to kill this docile creature.

The homeowner called the local police, but they had no equipment with which to capture the barn owl. She then called the Department of Environmental Conservation, but was told that unless the bird was sick or injured, they could do nothing to remedy the situation. Next, she called the local animal shelter, but was told they didn't handle wildlife calls. This infuriated the woman.

As darkness approached, the children finally left. The frightened owl somehow slipped away into the night, bruised and battered but miraculously still alive.

Shaken by the previous day's events, the frustrated woman continued to seek help for the owl, though she did not know where it had hidden. She made several inquiries at work and then contacted Mary Lou and me. She even called the newspaper, determined to convey her story of utter disappointment that no agency would help this wild bird. She told the reporter about our organization, making the point that as small and private as we were, our members would be willing to help out if the owl found itself in similar circumstances again.

The reporter asked for our names and phone numbers. Mary Lou was interviewed, giving a detailed account of the barn owl's nesting habits, food, nocturnal hunting activities as well as the steps we could take to help out, if the need arose.

When the article appeared in the newspaper the day after the interview, the headline, "Area Rehabilitators Want To Know Of Owl Sightings," caused our telephones to ring at all hours of the night with calls from residents living near the old factory where the owls' nests had been.

We received calls from insomniacs who counted owls instead of sheep; bar patrons on their way home from closing the neighborhood grills, and a 4:00 a.m. call from a bowling alley manager who spotted the owls on the building's tower, which was their regular perching spot and a sight he saw every night on his way home from work.

"You'll need a scaffold to get up to the towers," he said.

"Are the birds injured?" I inquired.

"Oh no. I see them in that same spot every night. I read that newspaper article so I thought you'd want to know if anybody spotted those owls," he replied.

"As long as they're OK, then we'll leave well enough alone," I said.

"I think there's a couple of nests up there," the caller said.

"Well, thanks for calling," I said.

"Do you want me to keep you up-to-date on them?" he asked.

"Only if they're in trouble, please!" I stressed.

None of the calls were crank calls, but none of them were emergency calls either. The birds were in no way distressed. They were going about their normal hunting jaunts and enjoying the night's relatively peaceful atmosphere. However, the newspaper article did state that we were anxious to know of owl "sightings". Mary Lou and I would pay dearly for this misquoted bit of information. What we really said was that if anyone in the vicinity saw the owls injured or sick or being mistreated again, we were available to rescue the birds. We wanted the public to know that someone cared, and that our volunteer organization was willing to help.

The result was two nights of interrupted sleep, followed by days of zombie-like behavior. Our patience was tested to the limit since those who called seemed long-winded, wide awake and oblivious to the time of night that they were calling. Besides, my heart would no sooner recover from its frantic, panic-induced beating, when I would fall back to sleep only to be shaken once again by the phone's ring exploding in my ear. Having my telephone by the bedside had its disadvantages. You know as well as I that calls in the middle of the night only signaled bad news. At least in past years that's all they had meant! My body could not adjust to this new sleeping disorder known as "WUASUR" (Wake Up and Shake Up Rehabilitators). The second night's onslaught of calls was no less jolting to my heart or my blood pressure. By the third day, the calls had stopped. In fact, the owls were never seen again. I would venture to guess that they all moved to a new location, finding a nesting site less visible to the public.

Late night phone calls were not exclusive to the barn owl story. Furthermore, I don't think that the telephone was invented to call a rehabilitator at 4:25 in the morning to inquire about the habits of an opossum. Believe it or not, that was the purpose of a call to me several months after the owl sightings.

A woman living in a nearby city saw an opossum on her back porch. She called the police first and they referred her to me. Just because my name was on file at the police station did not mean that she shouldn't consider what time it was!

She made no apologies for waking me up, but went into a dissertation on the activities of a nightly visitor, Mr. Opossum. She was surprised to see an opossum living in her urban area. She questioned why this creature was coming to her porch. Could it harm her two cats or could they hurt the opossum?

I asked if she put cat food on her porch. She admitted that she did put out food to feed neighborhood strays. I suggested, having listened to her describe the layout of her backyard, that she put the dishes of food at the far end of her yard by a woodpile to discourage the opossum from coming to her porch. If any other animal tried to attack this non-aggressive mammal, it could retreat to the safety of the woodpile.

The talkative caller explained that she didn't sleep much at night. Instead, she read and did some writing. That's how she came to notice the animal every night.

After about twenty minutes of conversation I told her that my nights were best used for sleeping, and bid her sweet dreams.

. . . something she had stolen from me!

Chapter Sixteen

American Kestrel Chicks

My first and only experience hatching eggs came after four years of raising nestlings and fledglings. Tiny and dependent as all orphaned baby birds are, nothing could compare to the responsibility I felt as I listened to the peeping going on inside the four American kestrel (sparrow hawk) eggs brought to me in the summer of '85.

A call came from a construction worker who was tearing down a building and had discovered a nest of hawk eggs. He was able to identify them as kestrels because the parents were buzzing the area trying to save their nest of soon-to-be-hatched young. But the man thought it best to remove the nest from the building and bring it home. He felt that there were too many people and too much activity in the immediate area.

He put the nest in a box and placed it in his truck to bring home later in the day. He knew enough to keep them warm until he found a rehabilitator who knew what to do for them.

His attempts to find help were unsuccessful that night, so he kept the eggs under a lamp by his bedside. All night long he and his wife could hear peeping inside **one** of the eggs. Sure enough, by dawn's early light, a chick, no bigger than a human thumb, was hatched. Now an all-out effort was made to locate a rehabilitator. After he had contacted every animal agency in the area, it was the police who gave the couple my name and number.

To be truthful, I didn't hold out much hope for the kestrels, since their natural parents would not be raising them during the most critical stage of their development. The gentleman was so enthusiastic and totally optimistic about their survival, that I gave in and told him to get the eggs and chick to me right away.

I was in the midst of an already hectic morning, feeding 18 baby gray squirrels, four young screech owls and several injured adult birds, The thought of setting up a homemade incubator and researching the books to learn the steps in success-fully raising kestrel chicks seemed too much to handle. Being unprepared complicated things enough to make the situation that much more stressful.

My mother came to the rescue, as usual. She helped me with the immediate feeding chores. She changed towels and papers in the tanks and cages while I set up a ten-gallon tank with a 100-watt bulb clamped overhead. I placed a heating pad under the tank to supplement the warmth from the bulb. Inside the tank I put a "nest" made of two quart berry baskets, taped together making a large enough nest to accommodate five chicks. In the baskets I put wash cloths. They would be easy to change as the need arose. The coarseness of the cloth would give the chicks something to cling to, preventing their legs from splaying. Slippery surfaces are not good for birds, especially in the growth development stage.

It would be necessary to monitor the temperature inside the tank. For that I used a thermometer that came from an old science kit that I had in my classroom.

Mr. Multonado arrived just as we were regulating the temper-ature in the tank. His wife and two small children were with him, as he gingerly carried the nest of four eggs and chick to the incu-bator. The buff-colored eggs, minutely dotted in dark brown, seemed too tiny to be that of American kestrels. They were slightly larger than the eggs of a robin. If the chick hadn't been there in front of me, I never would have believed that this helpless raptor would be transformed, in time, to a hunter of small birds, grasshoppers, crickets, beetles, and spiders in summer and mice in winter. Once all the eggs had hatched, this dietary information was needed to create a healthy menu for these beautiful hawks.

My immediate concern was to make sure that the environment that I had created was conducive to the successful hatching of the remaining eggs. A constant 98° was vital to both eggs and chick.

If I placed my ear close enough to the eggs I could hear peeping inside. It is difficult to put into words how I felt at that moment. Never having experienced this miracle of nature (other than watching it on television), I knew there was no turning back now.

I worried about how soon to feed them and exactly what to feed them and how often. I wondered if I should rotate the eggs because somewhere in my mind there was a vague recollection of seeing it done on a nature program. I fretted about the necessity of aiding the struggling chicks as they emerged from the eggs, though somehow this didn't seem natural. My role was to be that of an observer.

I remembered meeting a raptor expert at a rehabilitation seminar several years earlier. Her telephone number was easy to locate, since she was a New York State rehabilitator and this information was on a state-wide list.

Unfortunately, I got a taped message so I left my name and number, hoping that she would return my call before the action started.

In the meantime, the first chick, now six hours old, needed to be fed. I devised a concoction of chopped beef heart, mealworms, insects, egg yolk, milk and bonemeal. The ingredients were pureed in a blender. The consistency was like that of liver paté, easily digested and full of nutrients.

One tap of the chick's beak was all that was needed to entice this voracious newborn to eat. Once its crop was full, it fell fast asleep. This white fluffball had settled in quite nicely to its new nest, not realizing how close it had come to never knowing the existence of life beyond its shelled walls.

My hopes of reaching Mary Forness, the hawk expert, before the rest of the chicks hatched were dashed as the second egg began to show signs of cracking. Mom and I were joined by two more excited observers: Ken Gower, a friend and mechanic who had come to pick up mom's car for some repair work, and Lillian Deeb, the friend who had joined us on my first trip to Berne. They, too, were fascinated by the hatching. In their honor, the next two chicks would be their namesakes, despite the fact that all the chicks turned out to be males. I snapped pictures of the memorable event, which took thirty minutes from the first telltale crack to the emergence of the chick. It was excruciatingly difficult not to intervene and speed up the process by separating the two halves of the egg. I was strong though, taking photos while encouraging the chicks with words rather than actions.

The chick had what's called an egg tooth. It's a tiny bony protrusion on the tip of its upper beak. This is only visible for the first two days and then disappears, since the chick uses it exclusively for cracking the egg's shell. That wet hatchling seemed even smaller than its sibling, but once the white down dried it looked like its twin.

By mid-afternoon the third chick had made its entrance. We were no less awestruck by this event, but at least this time we knew what to expect. It was hard to concentrate on the feeding schedules of the other animals in our care. We didn't want to leave the kestrels for a minute, fearing we'd miss the next curtain call.

The fourth chick seemed to be as healthy as the others, but it died about four hours later.

The fifth egg never hatched at all. There had been peeping going on inside for about a day so we were confident that it would survive. When we could no longer hear any sounds and saw no movement of the egg, we knew that our little family of kestrels would number three.

I suspect that when I lowered the temperature in the incubator to accommodate the needs of the chicks who were now overheated, I should have isolated the last egg in a much warmer atmosphere of another incubator. Experience is a wonderful teacher. Maybe in nature, this last chick would not have hatched, either. There seems to be a fifty percent survival rate in the wild, so we were beating those odds. Mary returned my call a day later. I gave her all the details of my set-up as well as the recipe that was fed to them every hour. She recommended that I take frozen mice, which were always on hand in our wildlife freezer, remove the heads, legs and tails, put them through a meat grinder and feed it to the kestrels every two hours. I was also told to decrease the temperature in the incubator ever so slightly each day until it reached 78 degrees.

Mary gave me many other tips, words of caution and a great deal of moral support. We kept in touch as the need arose. To my surprise and delight, things went smoother than had been anticipated. The birds ate alternate meals of mice and the blended paté. After their crops were filled, they began preening themselves in order to get their feathers in perfect condition. This was a sign of well-being and contentment. To our astonishment, they regurgitated a pellet of bone and fur at only three days old. This meant that their digestive systems were working normally. All birds of prey need bone and fur to aid in digestion.

Mom had the unenviable task of grinding up the mice every morning while I fed the hungry squirrels. We took care of all the animals before eating breakfast ourselves. We were like zombies first thing in the morning, but quickly jumped into action after scanning the clinic tanks and cages making sure that everybody survived the night.

For the first few weeks of the kestrels' lives, I made it a habit to go downstairs in the middle of the night to check on them. I even fed them to make sure that they were not lacking proper nutrition. That extra feeding gave me a few minutes more sleeping time in the morning. The 6:15 a.m. feeding came soon enough!

As the kestrels grew, the clinic was filling up with wildlife orphans of every kind. Four little screech owls came at different times but were generally the same size and age, so I put them together. This was an ideal situation because they would be much less likely to become imprinted on me. Since none of them were injured or sick, I did not think it necessary to isolate them from the others. The owls found it very entertaining to watch the kestrels at the opposite end of the room. They were a number of weeks older and curious about everything.

The clinic room could not be used for both birds of prey and song birds. My basement kitchen and living room now became the clinic annex. As the kestrels kept pouring in that summer, I had to have more cages built to house them until they could be put outside in the flight cage. All the raptors thrived on this set-up. When it came time to transfer them outside, I was able to put the four screech owls in the flight cage adjacent to the three kestrels that we had hatched. I introduced two more kestrel fledglings to this compatible group.

The floor of the flight cage was covered with clean builder's sand. The insects and meal worms that crawled around there made a natural setting for the kestrels to learn how to hunt for their food. The birds played like children in a sand box. As their down feathers began to fall out, the birds played a game of pouncing on the feathers as the breezes pushed them around the cage floor.

At six weeks old, they were completely independent birds requiring little attention from me. I noticed their occasional restlessness. The owls, however, were slower in both growth and perceptual development. Their flight feathers took forever to grow in, unlike the kestrels whose adult feathers were fully visible at five weeks old. In fact, at three weeks old, the gray primary feathers clearly identified all our hatchlings as males.

When it came near the time for the kestrels' release, I started scouting around for the best place to set them free. Field and pastures would be ideal for them since they hover overhead, sometimes almost stationary for several minutes, scanning the ground below for the insects and mice that they catch and eat. I was lucky enough to find such a place not far from my home. This convenient setting would make it possible to check on the kestrels every day, just in case they still needed supplemental feedings from me. If they had become imprinted on me, the sound of my voice would bring them flying to me, looking for a hand-out of food. I doubted this would happen because during the weeks they stayed in the flight cage, none of the kestrels wanted to be hand fed. I only entered the cage to change their water, leave the food and rake up their droppings. They were curious about my activity, but stayed a good distance away. When the big day arrived to give them their freedom, I had a hard time catching them to put them in transport boxes. The sight of the net frightened them. Each bird gave me a run for my money as I attempted to catch him without doing any harm. All these weeks of trust that had developed between us quickly disappeared as I approached them with the net. At least I was reassured that they would probably fear other humans, too.

We do wild animals no favors by making pets out of them. Even if it is only a temporary situation, their chances of surviving in the wild are greatly lessened if we take away the most vital instinctual characteristic that they possess: fear of man.

As I drove to the release sight, an abandoned ski resort, I grew a bit anxious. It would be a bitter-sweet day for me, as every release day seemed to be. Deep in my heart, I knew that they were ready for their freedom. Yet I had become so attached to them that it was difficult to let them go, sensing that this would be my last contact with them. They were not going to hang around the property as the songbirds might do since I was releasing them miles away from my sanctuary. I couldn't release them in my backyard, because they would more than likely cause havoc among the other birds.

I think that a rehabilitator's greatest strength must be their willingness to part with the animals. This is not an easy sacrifice, but it is a pure one. It was with mixed emotions that I approached the entrance to the site.

Mom came along for moral support again and to have the thrill of seeing them fly uninhibited, no longer constrained by the limits of the aviary.

The release spot seemed perfect. The sun was shining, the breeze was mild. The weather forecast promised three days of moderate temperatures with no rain predicted.

I opened the two carriers, talking to the kestrels the whole time. It was not only my way of keeping the birds calm, but it seemed to be my way of comforting myself.

The birds were out of the boxes in a matter of seconds, taking flight immediately. They rose to heights far beyond our expectations. They circled above us, taking advantage of the wind currents. Their diet had made them strong! The birds called to one another and then flew toward a cluster of trees just beyond our view. We waited for about ten minutes, hoping to see them once more. Only one kestrel flew into sight, landing on the top of a telephone pole, flicking his tail up and down, so typical of this specie.

The kestrels' presence upset all the local birds. The barn swallows and goldfinches seemed particularly disturbed. We thought it best to leave. Our birds had afforded us the ultimate "high" in rehabilitation. Now it was time to say "good-bye" and go back to the other animals who still needed us.

I returned to the release site later that same day and three days in succession but never saw or heard them. I called to them each day, hoping to get one last glimpse of their beauty and grace. That was not to be. They had made a clean break.

When I released other falcons there weeks and months later, kestrels greeted them as the birds were introduced to the area. I saw no aggressive behavior, so there was a good chance that these birds were immature kestrels not territorial enough to chase my newly released birds out of the area. More important, they just might have been my three males.

Chapter Seventeen

A Duck of Notoriety

On a wind-chilled day in November, just after returning from shopping in Clifton Park (a suburb community about eight miles from my home), a call came from the Channel 6 TV Mobile Unit. Reporter Tom Mailey and his videographer were on the scene at a local Shop 'n Save Plaza in Clifton Park where they had been called by concerned employees. Tom told me that the WRGB "Tips" phone line had been used to try to get assistance for a mallard duck that seemed to be stranded in a recently frozen pond adjacent to the supermarket. Many ducks had spent the spring and summer there, but had left once a coating of ice had formed on the pond. This lonely duck seemed helpless out in the middle of the ice. Perhaps it was injured. To compound the problem, local children were now harassing the duck by throwing rocks and soda cans at it to force it to move.

When Tom first arrived to check out the situation, he quickly realized that some professional rescue efforts would be needed to save the duck. He contacted a veterinary clinic several blocks away, which in turn directed the reporter to me. Our conversation consisted of basic questions and answers, at which time I said that I would do what I could to rescue the mallard. With my sidekick (my mom), we gathered up our gear and drove back to Clifton Park. Earlier, we had been dressed for shopping. Now we were dressed in work clothes, high boots, heavy protective gloves, extension poles and nets to accessorize our outfits!

The pond resembled a lagoon not more than two feet deep. The ice was very thin. As I approached the duck with a loaf of bread in one hand and a net in the other, the ice broke. **"NO PROBLEM."** Well, a slight problem. The duck didn't fly to shore but instead waddled quite nicely to the opposite end of the pond. I then walked around the pond to approach the duck and that clever mallard once again waddled to the other side. So after a half hour of playing. "Catch me if you can!," a large crowd had gathered to watch this "fast breaking news story."

A very brave young woman offered to assist me by climbing down a stone embankment and leading the duck to me. She wore only sneakers whereas I was wearing hip boots. She knew that she would break through the ice into the frigid water. Nevertheless, she proceeded to join the rescue efforts.

Every step precipitated cracking the ice. After some daring maneuvers, the duck headed toward me and then darted away. My net barely touched the ungrateful, wayward duck and the process would start all over again. Finally, through some sleight of hand on my part, my trusty net swung over the whole body of the mallard and the capture was made. The crowd cheered and the momentous moment was recorded on tape for the "News at 6:00" with Tom Mailey and anchor, Liz Bishop.

Initial examination at the scene showed no apparent injuries. The duck was in good body weight and had healthy feather development. There were no parasites which might cause her to be in a weakened state. This led me to believe that she was a youngster that just got left behind.

Tom took some information from me so that he could come and visit our facility to do a follow-up story on the duck's progress. We then all left the rescue site and Mom and I took our little ward to the Lansingburg Veterinary Hospital, just around the corner from my home. Dr. Ron Scharf gave her a complete examination and concurred with me that she was in excellent health.

The news report that night prompted lots of attention and inquiries. Tom and his cameraman came the following day and the mallard put on quite a show swimming around in our kiddie pool set up in the clinic. She would dive under the water, swim around the perimeter and preen herself all for the camera. Tom asked me to bring the duck to the news studio for an interview with me, and to introduce the duck on their live news report. He also thought the celebrity duck should have an official name. So a "Name the Duck" contest was set up to let the viewers call in during the news program and vote on four names chosen as most popular during a postcard mail-in several days before the duck came to the studio. The choices were: Waddles, Groucho, Charduck (after Channel 6 Political Analyst Alan Chartock) and Lucky. With nearly 2,000 calls being made, "Charduck" was the winning name by a very narrow margin. Both the duck and

Professor Chartock were good sports. The mallard became an instant star. The duck had her own fan club of viewers who enjoyed the three nights of news. In the end, the spirit of cooperation and concern for one little duck raised the level of consciousness. It wasn't just a "Name the Duck" contest. It was a community that embraced a happy news story; a community whose members stopped to help a wayward duck and wasn't ashamed to admit it.

Charduck eventually was released on a pond at the Berkshire Bird Paradise Nature Center, about 20 miles from home. When she was ready, she could leave on her own or stay with the many other ducks that live there and are fed by the curator, Pete Dubacher. She deserved her freedom. It was up to her to choose the big day. After all, she was a celebrity and entitled to all the pampering she could get!

Little did I know that this media event was only the beginning of a very unusual series of winter rescues that more than matched this adventure.

Chapter Eighteen

The Bridge of My Discontent

Several days after the duck had been featured on the three news programs, a new story started to develop that would test me to the limits of my abilities both as a rehabilitator and a communicator. As a volunteer wildlife rehabilitator, one can expect unusual situations to occur because man and animals meet forces in unconventional ways. We then see the end results of these encounters. Although we try to remedy a problem on our own, sometimes the complexities of a situation dictate that many other people must get involved.

The story begins with a simple telephone call from a gentleman, Tom Turley from Lansingburgh, where I was born and have lived all of my life. He had been out on his daily walk which included crossing the 112th St. Bridge that spans the Hudson River between North Troy and the city of Cohoes. This old draw bridge, with its four towers in the center, was in disrepair but open to heavy traffic. It was not used as a draw bridge any longer because the mechanisms used to open it were frozen closed. Though it was maintained by the State of New York, only one person in the State Waterways and Bridge System had a key to open the tower doors. At one time, the maintenance men who opened and lowered the bridge stayed in the towers and were warmed by an old-fashioned wood stove inside. The rooms at the base of the towers were small and the chimneys extended upwards 25 to 30 feet. This made the towers, which enclosed the chimneys, seem very inviting to birds.

Mr. Turley noticed that several birds were trapped inside a room at the tower's base. They had fallen through the chimney into this windowed room and were banging into the glass panes frantically trying to get out. Traffic flowed continuously over the bridge but the commuters never noticed these birds. It wasn't until someone walked over the bridge that their plight was apparent.

Tom told me that he had seen me on television with the mallard duck and so I was the logical person to call to rescue them. He wasn't sure how long the birds had been in the tower room, but without food and water, they would surely die. Where does one begin to contact the right people to get access to this building? I told Tom that I would drive over and take a look at the situation.

I had to park on the Cohoes side of the bridge and then walk to the center of the span. It was mid November and winter had already arrived with bitter cold and naturally high winds swirling around the elevated structure. As I came upon the small windows, I saw eight starlings flying around inside and trying desperately to get out. I had hoped that a glass pane was broken and I could guide the birds out through the opening, but the windows were intact. There were dead birds in the opposite tower room. Their fight for life was lost. The doors were not only locked but rusted. If there was a key available, would it even work? As I stood on that bridge, the traffic was quite heavy, each vehicle adding more force to an already gusty wind. The dirt and dust particles were swirling around my face and the cold air made it difficult to catch my breath. At that point, I knew that I had my work cut out for me.

While walking back to my car, my mind was filled with all sorts of questions about how to get help for these trapped creatures. I don't even remember the ride home because my head was filled with scenarios on what to do next.

The telephone directory sure got a lot of use that day. There were so many state and municipal numbers to call. To make matters worse, Cohoes authorities said that Troy was responsible for the bridge and Troy authorities said that Cohoes was responsible. Each state number that I called referred me to another number. After ninety minutes of telephone hop-scotch, I finally was put in touch with Mr. Dave Cox, Department of Transportation's Head Engineer for Bridge and Waterway Maintenance, who then contacted the only man available with the key to the bridge's towers. I was told to meet Bob Hodge at the bridge in two hours. What we all thought would be a simple plan of action turned out to be a two-month-long nightmare.

I met Bob Hodge at a convenience store on the Troy side of the bridge. As we walked to the center of the span, Bob told me that the bridge had not been manned in many years, since the structure had been permanently removed from the list of bridges that opened up to large boats. It was, however, a vital link between two cities and thousands of vehicles passed over it every day. The tower rooms were just used for some storage but otherwise were unoccupied.

When we reached the room on the north side of the bridge, Bob inserted the key into the lock, struggled to turn the key, pushed and pulled on the doorknob and after quite a struggle, the door opened, to our relief. Expecting the birds to fly out into the sunshine, we met instead with their disappearance up through the remnants of a dropped ceiling that had partially collapsed to the floor. Their fear of humans and the sound of passing traffic had sent them upward into the tower's chimney section. Stepping into the room, we peered up into the tower and saw that the starlings were perched on metal rods that protruded from the brick tower structure. The chimney hole was just large enough for the birds to fall in but too small and menacing for them to want to escape.

Our next plan of action was to leave the door open, stand a few feet away and hope that the birds would fly back down and use the opened door with the sun's rays pouring in as a guide to their freedom. After about 15 minutes, two birds flew down into the room only to be frightened back up into the tower by the noise of the cars. This back and forth behavior continued for two hours. Bob had another assignment to cover so I told him I would stay for the rest of the day to set these birds free. He needed to take the key but that meant that I wouldn't be able to lock up when I left the site. It was decided that he would return in three hours so I was stuck there no matter what transpired in the meantime. My modus operandi would be to stand by the door of the kiosk-size tower room and watch to see if any of the dozen or so birds found their way out.

As I watched Bob walk over the bridge to his truck, I was hopeful that the next time we saw each other the rescue effort would be completed. How wrong I was.

From my vantage point right next to the door, I was unable to see what was going on in the room. I decided to cross to the other side of the bridge and watch the activity from there. For longer periods of time than I care to remember, the room looked empty. Then one bird descended from the ceiling followed by a second, then two more and finally eight or nine would fill the room. Just as my hopes of freedom would soar, traffic would whiz by, sending the birds whirling inside the building, before disappearing up through the hole in the dropped ceiling again.

This same reaction repeated itself, as if taken from a bad dream that haunts our sleep on a regular basis. Only this was not a dream, but a rehabilitator's nightmare. For three hours, I watched the birds' plight. They were within inches of the open sky, only to be frightened back to the top of the tower by the noisy traffic. When I entered the room to observe their condition, I was also able to shelter myself from the bitter cold that numbed my face, fingers and toes.

As it started to near 4:00 p.m., the sky darkened and a new plan of action had to be devised. The sun no longer was the birds' guide. They were now settled in for the night way up in the tower's uppermost interior ledges. Only two birds had found their way out in the five hours that I had spent there. I waited for Bob to return and asked him to stay a little longer so that I could run home to get food and water to leave in the birds' prison, which might extend their lives at least till I returned.

When the door was locked for the night, Bob and I made arrangements to meet the next morning so that I could spend the day on the bridge. Needless to say, I was exhausted and discouraged. Perhaps the next day would be better. A hot shower and a good meal followed by a good night's sleep would recharge my spirit.

As planned, Bob met me for coffee at 9 a.m. sharp. He handed me the key, wished me luck and reminded me that the door would have to be locked whenever I left the bridge because of liability concerns. In fact, I had to sign a waiver form that freed the state of any responsibility if I were to be injured while on the bridge during the performance of this rescue.

As I walked to the towers, I wondered how many more birds had fallen into the room through the chimney overnight. The chimneys on both towers were roosting places and the wind might have blown them into the chimney's hole. If only the towers had been capped.

I inserted the key into the hole. I felt my heart pumping through my double layers of clothing. I could see many birds fluttering around inside as I peered through the window. But the key wouldn't turn. I pushed and pulled at the rusted door, struggled to turn that key; pushed my shoulder up against the door and tried to turn the key again.

"Lord," I said in a whisper. "Please help me get this key to work."

Cars kept on rushing by, some people honking their horns. Maybe they recognized me from seeing me there the day before. The irony was that I never felt more alone in my whole life. Hundreds of cars passed in the 20 minutes that I struggled with the key. Yet there was no one but me to open that door! With this in mind, I gave the key one last chance to turn and felt half the key move while the other inserted half remained fixed.

"Uh oh. This isn't happening," I cried. Now I had gotten myself in a predicament. "Stay calm. Don't panic. So what if this is the only key in New York State that fits this door!" I slowly bent the top half of the key back to its original position, said a little prayer and tried to pull the key out in one piece. It wouldn't budge. I needed pliers. So I walked back to my car where I had a tool kit and returned with the pliers. I struggled another few minutes and finally was able to remove the key.

"What do I do now?" I said to myself. I decided to walk back again to the Cohoes side of the bridge where there was a factory with a business office, and call Bob Hodge. I walked into the office and began to explain my dilemma. The office staff didn't quite know how to take my explanation, but allowed me to use their telephone directory and phone. Bob did not answer the phone at his post at the Green Island Bridge, which was down river about three miles. I called several other numbers but got nowhere.

I decided to drive to where Bob was scheduled to be, only to find his station locked and unmanned. This day was turning out to be worse than the day before.

Several blocks from the 112th Street Bridge was a hardware store. If they could make new copies of this key, I'd be in luck. With great anticipation and anxiety I entered Manupella's Hardware and Supply Store, showed the owner the key and in less than five minutes, I walked out with three new keys! I didn't know whether these second, third and fourth generation keys would work but with no other options available, I took the bull by the horns and returned to the bridge of my discontent.

Having parked my car on the Cohoes side, I walked **back** over the bridge with the wind pushing me, hurrying me along as if there was no time left to save those birds. Would the keys work? In a matter of seconds I had my answer.

The key fit into the slot. The birds were banging on the window and the traffic still continued to throw dirt in my face! I turned the key slowly to the right, a little at a time, as I pushed myself against the door. The knob was rigid. Then, I pulled as hard as I could, the door opened with a burst of force strong enough to send me flying backward and the birds flying up through the ceiling. I didn't care. I was willing to wait all day for the poor things to calm down, letting the fresh air from the open door guide them out.

Hours passed with fewer than three or four birds finding their way out. I was cold and bored. I found myself observing every inch of my surroundings. I prayed. I counted the trees along the river's shoreline, bereft of leaves on this bitter November day.

As nightfall approached, I locked the door, aware of the birds that were still trapped inside. Their numbers were sure to increase by morning as those roosting on top of the uncapped chimney became the next victims.

Just as I thought, the third day on the bridge was as tedious and cold as the previous ones. Now I was starting to recognize motorists who beeped at me. The pedestrians who braved walking over the bridge daily had come to know of my rescue attempts. They found it interesting, but went on their way with the complacency that I found perplexing. Their detachment from the situation made them able to continue on over the bridge, never giving the plight of these creatures a second thought.

Hot coffee and sandwiches kept me going for six long weeks. It was really a losing battle because the chimney was like a vacuum system sucking in the birds on a regular basis. A decision to stop visiting the bridge was close at hand. I had made my daily visits through Thanksgiving, then Christmas and into January. The snow made the walk across the bridge treacherous. I couldn't take the below-freezing temperatures much longer.

When I spoke to the state authorities about having the chimneys capped, their answer was that there was a long list of repairs that had to be done on many other waterway projects and that capping two chimneys to save birds at this time was not financially justified.

My own life was put on hold for all these many weeks. I had to walk away from that bridge after the seventh week, brokenhearted that many birds would probably die an agonizing death because a bureaucracy and all its tax-supported employees couldn't take a few hours to help a highly taxed citizen.

About a week after I had decided not to return to the bridge, I read in the local paper that our assemblyman was working with Niagara Mohawk Power Company to have lights installed on the 112th Street Bridge. His constituents had been asking for years to have lights for safety and security. This was the possible solution to ending the two-month-long journey of frustration. Why not install the new lights and cap the chimneys at the same time, with the use of a bucket truck? So I called Assemblyman Neil Kelleher's office and explained the whole story to him. He told me to be patient. He'd get back to me by the end of the day.

Assemblyman Kelleher spent a good portion of the day coordinating a plan that included Niagara Mohawk, the Dept. of Transportation and Volunteers For Distressed Wildlife to get this problem corrected once and for all. Within twenty-four hours, all four tower chimneys were capped, including the ones that had not been a problem. To watch the last screen being placed on the chimney was such a moment of satisfaction for me.

We all went our separate ways that day. We have had no reason to meet on that bridge again. I do drive across it on a regular basis, but for me the trip holds unique memories. Those memories have given way to a newly constructed bridge that was started about four years after my encounter. It's a beautiful structure, minus the towers I had come to hate. There are no chimneys or rooms. The wind still howls and the river's bends and turns remain the same. There are now condominiums along the river's western shoreline. The trees that I had counted are now gone.

Chapter Nineteen

I Kept My Promise

When you spend so much time trying to lesson the pain and suffering of animals, whether it be through their actual medical treatment or the unending letter-writing campaigns to promote protective animal legislation, it makes complacency among humans that much more difficult to accept.

Even more dangerous is the lack of sensitivity toward these creatures who cause us no harm, pose no threat and most of all, have no way of self protection from man's cruelty.

Though I know next to nothing about fish, a particular experience touched me so profoundly that I feel compelled to record what my mind cannot erase.

While vacationing and volunteering at a wildlife center on Sanibel Island, Florida, I came upon a fishing pier jutting out into the bay. I could see many locals as well as tourists enjoying the sunshine and calm weather. Those who were fishing had no trouble casting their lines out into an aqua-colored sea. It was a perfect day. Sanibel Island is a nature lover's paradise with half the island preserved for wildlife habitation. Most everyone who lives there or visits has an elevated respect for its natural beauty. I felt right at home, or so I thought. As I approached the pier to take photographs of the brown pelicans, I inhaled the wonderfully fresh air that only the salt of the ocean can offer. Every person I had met during my stay had been a nature and animal lover, so I was not prepared for the harsh reality that was to come.

The pelicans floating near the pier were waiting for hand-outs from the fishermen. Terns and gulls circled overhead in a cloudless sky. Egrets and herons perched on the railings just waiting for me to capture their images for my albums.

I shot a role of film, pausing only long enough to change the cartridge. Through my view finder I spotted a fisherman pulling up a string of fish to be prepared for a meal. To my horror, he was beginning to filet a **live** fish. His razor-sharp knife slowly separated the meat from the bones, evidently missing all vital organs, since the fish continued to gasp for air.

I said to him, "Wouldn't it be better if you killed the fish before you filet it?"

"Yes, I guess you're right." he replied.

Had I perhaps touched this man's sense of compassion?

Then he added, "But when you do ten or twenty of these . . . " his voice falling away.

"I can imagine," I answered.

Then the fisherman turned over the poor creature and proceeded to continue his precise carving method, devoid of hesitation or conscience. The fish stayed alive, flapping its tail, sucking in the air through its gaping mouth and gills. Then in an act of questionable mercy, the fish butcher tossed his capture into the bay where a hungry pelican was able to end what the fisherman had begun.

Two thin filets were placed in a plastic bag. It was just another day for that fisherman, but I was left shaken by the event. Sadly, I was the only one who even took notice. I wondered what made all of us so different. Now misty eyed, I could not focus clearly enough to take more photos, nor could I ever return to the pier.

Cruelty comes in many forms. I have concluded that it is always combined with a cowardly act. Perhaps they go hand in hand. Another such act of cowardice came in the month of June, about six months after I had returned from my trip to Sanibel Island. The warm summer air was just returning to the northeast, so this certainly was not the time for people to be using their fireplaces. Why, then, would a person need to light a fire to force out a mother raccoon and her five newborns from a chimney? Mrs. Raccoon was only there to raise her young. Once they were old enough, they would venture out, and the homeowner could then cap the chimney. Even if his intention was to smoke them out of the chimney, he would have killed them due to the effects of smoke inhalation.

This episode started with a telephone call from the Cohoes Police Department. A resident on the Columbia Street Extension said that someone had abandoned kittens on his front lawn. This street is a busy main thoroughfare, so the kittens were in danger. The police sent the Animal Control Officer to the scene to rescue them and take them to the Mohawk Hudson River Humane Society. When she arrived, there were no kittens but instead she found five screaming baby raccoons. Their eyes were still sealed shut. There was no sign of their mother, which is why they were so cold. The box that they had been dumped in had a strong odor of smoke. As the control officer picked each one up, they too smelled of smoke and also had a layer of soot on their tiny bodies. It was quite clear that she needed the assistance of a wildlife rehabilitator. A phone call from the dispatcher alerted me to the officer's imminent arrival, so I immediately prepared a formula, a heating pad and filled the double sink in my clinic with warm water to clean the babies. There were baby skunks, squirrels, dozens of nestling birds and even three abandoned kittens already here in the nursery. I didn't know if I could handle five more helpless babies, but I couldn't turn them away either. When the adrenaline is pumping, you act on the moment. Then when things calm down, you assess the task of caring for all these hungry, needy babies and you ask yourself, "What have I gotten myself into?" Thank God for my mother's help.

When the control officer arrived, she explained her suspicions that the man who called about the kittens had cleverly suckered her into taking away what he considered to be **nuisance animals.** The hook was to think she was rescuing kittens, but once she arrived to find these wild animals, she would have no choice but to take them away. He must have been so proud of his deceitful plan.

When I opened the box to examine the babies, I was horrified to find that they all had been burned. The severity of their injuries was so great that I immediately called our Lansingburgh Veterinary Hospital to see if I could bring the raccoons there for treatment. I was hopeful that I could save three of them but it was doubtful whether the other two had a chance for recovery. I firmly believe that undue suffering is not acceptable, so I was ready to make the hard decision of euthanasia if the doctor and I agreed that they would suffer needlessly, only to die after many weeks of treatment. Rehabilitators must always take into consideration the fact that these animals must eventually be healthy enough to survive in the wild on their own. This is our ultimate goal. If their injuries leave them handicapped, chances of survival are dramatically reduced.

Within a half hour, Doctor Ron Scharf was examining the five raccoons. My initial observation of their conditions was right on target. The burns on three of them were treatable with ointments and antibiotics. They were not dehydrated. The fourth raccoon was moderately burned and if we could avoid an infection, his chances were good. The fifth baby was another story. He was much too critical to save, so I made the decision to end his suffering. I held him close to my heart as the drug took effect. It was peaceful and quick. There was little time for tears, as we jumped into action to treat the others' wounds.

Dr. Scharf sent me home with medications and a list of instructions. The raccoons were placed in their carrier and snuggled close to one another for warmth. My clinic would be the best place for 24-hour care. I could just roll out of bed, come downstairs and attend to their needs.

Mom anxiously awaited my return. As my car pulled into the garage, she could hear them screaming to be fed. This was an encouraging sound as it meant that their lungs had not been damaged by the smoke. Having to tell Mom that I had lost one youngster saddened us both. Our spirits were subdued. Yet we could not let ourselves show our true emotions, because the task at hand was to get the four surviving raccoons downstairs, settled in and fed.

I placed the raccoons in a large towel that had been warmed in the dryer. There was a heating pad under a cardboard box. The bottom of the box was lined with paper and another towel. As I placed them in the box, I noticed their burns looked raw, even though the doctor had treated each one.

I heated their formula as Mom began feeding all the other hungry, demanding babies in the nursery. The symphony of kitten, skunk, squirrel and bird sounds could not be ignored. Everybody was starving, even though they had been fed less than three hours before. In fact, the birds had just been fed right before my return, but the sound of our voices always excited them into thinking it was mealtime once again.

When the formula was the right temperature, I began to introduce each one to the preemie nipple that I knew would seem foreign to them. This was not mommy's teats! Each one rejected the bottle, biting the nipple and squirming to get away from this imposter who was doing a poor impression of a lactating female! This was not unexpected, since we had raised baby raccoons before. The added difficulty was that their burns made them irritable. I had to be extra careful not to touch the areas that were so tender.

After an hour of struggling, they were all satisfied enough to cuddle up to each other and quiet down. The combination of feeding and then stimulating each one to urinate was just what they needed to settle in for a nap. The silence was glorious. Now I began to hear a hint of purring in the box. This was music to my ears.

I tiptoed around their box, not wanting to make the slightest sound that would initiate another crying episode. The bottles and utensils were left soaking in the sink so as not to interrupt their slumber. All the other wards were now quiet as well, so Mom and I went upstairs to prepare dinner, which was already three hours later than usual.

Once before retiring and twice during the night, I came downstairs to feed the screaming babies. Mom joined me for the ll p.m. feeding to prepare formulas and fruits for the next day. This was our ritual. Sometimes I brought the raccoons upstairs to my bedroom because I couldn't face those stairs in the middle of the night. My legs and back were weakening. The fact that the clinic and nursery were in the basement was both a blessing and a curse.

When the raccoons were out of danger, Alice Brown, a volunteer who specialized in raccoons, took the four babies to her home. She could focus all her attention on them, which was not an option for me. They spent the entire summer and early fall with her. Her husband Don built a huge enclosure for them with a wading pool, trees to climb and a nesting box. They thrived in this setting. They were so healthy and beautiful that they became subjects for a local wildlife artist, Donna Mariano.

When it was time to release the raccoons, they each weighed over twenty-two pounds. It was a long way from the days when the little ones would barely fit in the palm of my hand. Their fur coats were luxurious from the healthy and natural diet that Alice and Don had given them. I had made sure that they were all inoculated against rabies. This was the best gift I could have given them, because a year or two after their release, an epidemic of rabies nearly wiped out the raccoon population in our area.

Don and Alice owned quite a bit of land about thirty-five miles north of us. They had put a trailer on the property. After clearing a bit of the land, a pond would be dug. The setting would be perfect for the raccoons. Don built a nesting box and placed it way up in a huge oak tree. If the raccoons didn't choose this spot for their home, there were plenty of other tree cavities available for immediate inspection. The property was well posted and Don and Alice visited there regularly to make sure the signs were obeyed.

The day before they were to be released, I went to visit them for the last time. As I approached their enclosure, I could see that they were growing restless, sticking their paws out the holes in the fencing. They wanted to have the freedom of the whole backyard. It was a perfect opportunity to be photographed with them as they climbed the wire, making a frame of their bodies encircling me. There was no hint of the burns that once had threatened their lives. I couldn't help but remember the one raccoon that would not be joining his siblings.

"I promise you, my beautiful raccoons, that your sibling will not be forgotten. I will name him 'Blaze'. I will write a poem in his memory and share his story with anyone who will listen," I whispered to them.

I waited all the next day to hear from Alice and Don. I envisioned how the raccoons would react to their freedom and the great outdoors. If I hadn't been so overwhelmed with the responsibilities of all the animals at my home, I would have joined my friends for this long-awaited day.

When the telephone rang for the thirty-first time that day, I was thrilled to hear Alice's voice. All had gone well. The raccoons loved their new surroundings. They explored every foot of acreage. Don and Alice stayed in the trailer for the weekend so they could monitor the raccoons' adjustment.

When it was time to leave, Don put out plenty of food. The property offered berries and fish from the brook that ran through the woods. Don had brought home crayfish for the raccoons while they were caged, so they were accustomed to catching and handling them in their kiddie pool. The brook would be more of a challenge, but they were ready.

It was tough driving away from their property. Don and Alice had grown attached to the raccoons. They tried to prepare themselves, but tears of joy and sadness were the order of the day. The anxiety began days before the appointed date. Now they worried about the raccoons' survival. I had known this feeling a thousand times before. It came with the territory, so to speak.

When Don checked the spot where he left food on a regular basis, every morsel of it was gone. Although it was impossible to know whether the raccoons or other animals on the property had eaten it, there were plenty of encouraging signs that our raccoons were enjoying the offerings. Their prints and droppings were easy to spot and identify.

Until the first snowfall, Don and Alice made their visits to the site. They were delighted to catch peeks of the raccoons in early evening when they were most active. I wasn't so lucky as to see them on my visit to the property, but the spot was so ideal that I just knew that they were fine.

It was now time to prepare for the long northeast winter that promised us some semblance of normalcy. As harsh as these winters usually are, we could manage to recharge our minds and bodies for the spring babies that would start to come our way the following March. After having released all the other animals by mid October, all of us welcomed the rest.

I kept my promise . . . .

In Memory of Blaze the Raccoon

I cried for you today little one,
as I held you in the palm of my hand.

Your little body quivered as I treated your burned
toes and legs.

I cried for you today little one,
as I bathed you to remove the soot and dead flesh.

Your nose and lips were raw from the flames that
came through the fireplace to force you out of
your safe and cozy home in the chimney.

I cried for you today little one,
for your eyes had not yet opened to see the
cruelty of this world.

I hope you know that this human,
whose tears moisten your tiny head,
tried her best to save you.

I cried for you today little raccoon,
because you died so young and unnecessarily.

Your habitat is being destroyed and your mother
had no place to build her nest.

You would be alive today if the chimney
had been capped.

It was a bittersweet day today little one,
as I held your four siblings in my arms,
gratified that they would survive.

You touched me in a very profound way little
one, and I just needed to say, "good-bye."

Chapter Twenty

Shorter Stories

Some of my stories are short and sweet. What they lack in quantity, they more than make up in quality. I like to refer to them as my "Shorter Stories."

It was a chilly day in March when my friend Margaret Gerighty called me to ask for my help. She had been hearing a chirping sound coming from her chimney. Convinced that a baby robin was in distress, she first asked the man across the street to check out the chimney and the heating system. The chirping had started the night before and continued the next day. Having moved in three months before, Margaret had a lot to learn about her new property.

Going on what Margaret had told him, John began to dismantle the heating system. He heard the same peeping sounds but the walls of the heater were triple lined, making it impossible to retrieve anything from its interior. Poor John was covered with soot. It was time to call the bird expert. It was my turn to solve the mystery.

I tried to explain to my friend that there were no baby robins or any other specie having babies in early March. The birds had not migrated north yet. Margaret insisted that there was a baby bird somewhere in her house. My common sense explanation did not soothe Margaret's heartfelt concern, so I told her that I'd pack up my equipment and come right over.

There was still snow on the ground as I drove to Margaret's house, just three blocks from my home. Baby birds are not born this early and they do not chirp after dark, so there was something very strange about this unidentified peeping sound. Past experience had taught me to expect the unexpected.

As soon as I walked into the living room and knelt down next to the large floor vent, it was apparent to me that John was still banging on the heating ducts. Not being able to hear the peeping, I yelled down to John to cease and desist the destruction of

Margaret's ventilation system! Within seconds, I heard the distinct sound of a smoke detector alarm, signaling the need to change its battery!

"Peep, peep."

"Did you hear that?" Margaret whispered as she knelt next to me.

"Is that the bird sound you've been hearing?" I asked through a veiled smile.

"That poor baby has been crying like that since last night. It must be so hungry," she said. "It kept me up all night."

I wanted to tell her right away that her smoke detector was the culprit but I waited until I heard the sound again. If I was able to find the location of the detector, I would have my proof.

"Peep, peep."

"There it is again," she insisted.

"Margaret, do you have a smoke detector in your house?"

"I'm not sure," she answered.

"Peep, peep."

The smoke detector was in the ceiling of the hallway leading to the bedrooms. Margaret never realized that it had been her protector all these months. The landlord of her previous apartment never installed detectors. Time to change the battery. Time to tell John the problem was solved.

"John, you can put the heater back together now," I yelled down the vent hole. "It was the smoke alarm."

John was mortified that he hadn't recognized the sound. It was a noise that he had heard many times before. It just proves that the power of suggestion is very strong. Once Margaret planted the suggestion in John's mind, the rest is history. Case closed for Sherlock Ziter!

It took ten years before a clutch of eastern bluebirds came my way. Many people had encouraged bluebirds to return to the area by putting up nesting boxes on their property. Frank and Rose Yank, a Voorheesville couple, joined in that effort by placing houses along the border of their backyard. They were rewarded with a nesting pair of our state's official bird.

The Yanks watched the parents prepare the nesting box, flying back and forth with materials found throughout the neighborhood. They counted the days until the five delicate eggs hatched. Then tragedy struck, when Frank found parts of the female's body scattered at the base of the house, the victim of a roaming feline.

Frank and Rose watched the nest all day long, hoping that the male would take over the feeding of the five newly hatched birds. There was no sign of the male. Every hour that passed brought the weakened hatchlings closer to death. They made the decision to call their local veterinarian. Like so many other referrals, the Yanks were given my name and number.

I thought it best to wait a bit longer before removing them from their box and bringing them to me. By nightfall, if the male was not sitting on the nest to keep the babies warm, I was standing by to accept the orphans.

Darkness brought disappointing news. The male had not assumed responsibility. He had not made an appearance all day long. The hatchlings were gathered up and delivered to me at nine o'clock that evening. The inch long, nude babies were my responsibility now! They were weak, chilled and barely alive. Their mouths were so tiny that I fed them with a toothpick. Because they were too weak to lift their heads, I propped up their necks with the fingers of my left hand while prying open their beaks with the toothpick in my right hand. Their eyes were sealed shut. The five birds filled a small matchbox. It was going to be a long night. I had to make up for the feedings that they had missed. If they had any chance at all, the next 24-hours were the most critical.

Each time I came downstairs to feed them, I expected to find one or two dead. To my great joy, all five showed improvement. They gained enough strength to lift their heads to accept the food, and each one showed its will to live by standing tall, stretching its neck to be the first to reach the toothpick. For the first five days, they were fed every fifteen minutes. Then they were able to wait until I came down to feed the other birds at thirty minute intervals.

In six weeks, after having graduated from the matchbox to a pint basket, then to a quart basket, on to a cage and finally to the outside aviary, release day was soon to follow. I released them on my sanctuary just in case they needed a few days of supplemental feedings. All the songbirds released here came back to us to be fed in the trees closest to the aviaries, gradually relying less on our handouts. The call of the wild made sure of that. Like those before them, the bluebirds followed the same pattern. Realizing that I had a hand in the resurgence of the eastern bluebird population was a "feather" in my cap! A bluebird feather, that is.

For as long as I can remember, my mother always had a special place in her heart for the beautiful red fox. When we moved into our new home in 1976, the first thing she asked for was a brass fox head door knocker. It took a long time before I was able to find one. My trip to the Adirondack Mountain region led me to Old Forge, New York, where the perfect door knocker was on display in a big hardware store. The minute I spotted it, I was determined to buy it. The fox head was screwed to a display board along with many other animal subjects from which to choose. The fox was the only one left of its kind. I convinced the store clerk to remove the display and sell it to me. This door knocker was perfect for our front entrance. Mom would have her fox.

Other than seeing a red fox in the wild, the door knocker was the closest we had ever been to a fox. That was until a five week old fox kit, found abandoned along an exit ramp of the Taconic State Parkway, 75-miles from our house, was brought to us.

A family from the Poughkeepsie area was making the trip to Albany to spend the weekend with friends. They spotted what they thought was a puppy on the side of the road. Their plan was to take the puppy along for the ride, hoping that their friends in Albany could relay the pup to an animal shelter. Observing the features of this animal lead them to question whether they were transporting a puppy or a fox to Albany.

They arrived at their destination with a hungry, screaming red fox demanding to be fed. Their hosts for the weekend decided to take the kit to the Animal Emergency Clinic, where the staff confirmed their suspicions. This was indeed a red fox. Next stop was The Animal Hospital in Guilderland. Dr. Ed Becker and his staff had many years of experience treating wildlife. Treating injured wildlife was one thing. Raising orphaned wildlife was another story. Enter the Ziters. The fox kit was about to take one more ride. A staff member from Dr. Becker's office brought the five week old male to us.

The white tip on his tail, his big ears and pointed face were all clues to his parentage. This precious bundle melted Mom's defenses. The amazing story of his circuitous journey to Troy was the defining moment when she accepted the challenge, ignoring her inner voice of better judgement. Mom was the one who kept my compass steady whenever I was tempted to accept animals not suited for our facility. The roles were now reversed. I hesitated to change her mind. This was a once-in-a-lifetime opportunity.

When I look at the door knocker, I am reminded of the three months that the fox spent with us. The learning experience was like no other. When it was time to release him, a fellow rehabilitator in Columbia County, close to where he had been found, let us release him on her 200-acre estate. The fox had come full circle. The compass pointed homeward.

Some birds build their nests in the darndest places. Many times those places turn into death traps for the young. The Starlite Theatre in Latham, a summer venue for live entertainment, was preparing the main theatre and outside patios for its Opening Night performance. With only two days left for the contractors and maintenance crews to get the stage and grounds in order, dozens of birds' nests filled with babies were found behind the main stage lights that were about to be tested. The woman in charge of the contractors ordered the work to be stopped until she was able to locate wildlife officials. She had been on the scene the year before when all the birds died as a result of being burned by these same lights. She was not about to let it happen under her supervision. The Conservation Department referred her to Volunteers For Distressed Wildlife and that's how Mom and I got involved.

Without delay, we rushed to the theatre to remove as many nests as we could and bring the nestlings home. The woman had mentioned that many other nests were in hanging flower baskets that decorated the outside patios and refreshment tents. Our plan was to relocate the baskets to the outer perimeter of the area, hoping to coax the parents to follow the cries of the nestlings and continue their care of the young.

The nests behind the stage lights were well hidden, 15 to 20 feet up in the eaves of the building. At first we only saw a telltale piece of straw or string hanging from the edge of the structure. A member of the construction crew climbed a ladder, enabling him to reach the set of lights to expose the rest of the nest. We waited below to collect the babies that he handed us. The boxes that we brought with us barely held all the babies. There were twelve stage lights with nests behind each one! Each nest held at least four babies. It was not easy keeping the birds confined to their nest and having the nest handed to us. Instead, the nests disintegrated as the lights were removed. The babies came down one at a time as we counted out loud, "1, 2, 3, 4 . . . 12, 13, 14 . . . " This was going to be a record breaking year for me! Luckily for us, most were eggs.

Next, we tackled the hanging plant dilemma. This did not pose too much of a problem, because we were able to let the parents watch us carry the pots to safer areas for them to continue to raise their clutches. All construction work was halted until our work was finished. The time clock was running so we moved expeditiously. The parent birds were understandably upset, but they followed us to the new sites, anxious to feed the chirping nestlings.

Back at the theatre, a wire mesh guard was made to prevent the birds from building nests in the eaves again. Then it was time to test the stage lights. All the colored spotlights worked. Safe in our boxes, the birds were spared a painful death. It was time to put the men back to work. The Starlite Theatre's refurbishing was on its way to completion.

The deadline was met. Opening Night was a success. I guess you could say that the Ziters played a part in that old adage, "The show must go on." I say that the hero in this story was the supervisor who stopped everything to find help for birds whose lives were worth saving.

On the night of January 3, 1991, a call from the dispatcher of the Rensselaer County Sheriffs Department set into motion a minute by minute rescue attempt that can best be described in this way.

4:30 p.m.
Volunteers For Distressed Wildlife receives the initial call from the dispatcher regarding a duck that is believed to be frozen in the ice on a reservoir at the top of Northern Drive, five minutes from my home.

4:32 p.m.
Troy Animal Control Officer Cathy Nealon gets a message that a duck is frozen on that same reservoir.

4:34 p.m.
Nealon calls Volunteers For Distressed Wildlife, requesting hip boots and our assistance. We agree.

4:48 p.m.
I arrive on the scene to locate the stranded duck, some 200 feet from shore. Visibility is poor. Darkness is approaching.

4:53 p.m.
Two Sheriff Deputies arrive after receiving a report that youngsters may be out on the ice. They find only me and the duck!

4:55 p.m.
Nealon arrives. She makes an attempt to walk across the ice. Too dangerous! Ice is barely an inch thick in spots. I insist that she consider other options.

4:59 p.m.
A concerned man drives to the scene to offer us his rubber dinghy. Officer Nealon volunteers to get in it and slide herself to the duck. The paddle will not work, so she propels the dinghy by masterfully using her rear, rocking back and forth, sending the raft forward in spurts, a foot at a time. Ropes have been attached to the dinghy beforehand to retrieve her.

5:10 p.m.

Nealon reaches the duck only to find that it is not frozen in the ice. Though injured, it hobbles away from her. She has no net!

5:20 p.m.

Deputies and other helpers pull Nealon back. She is given my extension net.

5:25 p.m.

Off goes Officer Nealon, sliding across the ice, inch by inch into the darkness with only our two flashlights to guide her. A State Trooper arrives to lend us more ropes so Nealon's "lifeline" can be extended.

5:35 p.m.

The duck is captured and brought back to shore where dozens of people have gathered to watch the rescue. I examine the duck. It has been shot.

5:45 p.m.

I bring the duck to my home to treat the wounds. The bullet made an entry and an exit hole.

7:00 p.m.

I take the duck to the Capital District Emergency Clinic, Latham, where Dr. Gregory Bayan and his staff treat the duck and keep it overnight.

7:00 a.m.

Friday. I pick up the duck to finish the rehabilitation at my home.

After several weeks of recuperation, the duck was adopted by Lee and Patty Hess, both Troy Police Officers.

This was one lucky duck!

Chapter Twenty-One

Crow Crow

Crow Crow was our mascot. He symbolized all that was good about our volunteer work. For six years he lived without knowing a moment of cruelty or even an unkind word. He never knew the pangs of hunger or faced competition for food. He enjoyed the freedom of flight, but chose to stay within the borders of our property. I think that he knew its boundaries from watching me mow the lawn every weekend.

He came to us after tumbling from a big evergreen tree on the campus of The College of St. Rose in Albany, New York. The fall caused several fractures. His right leg and wing must have taken the brunt of the impact. He was just three weeks old, so I hoped that the bones would heal. His injuries didn't curb his appetite. I suppose we spoiled him because he was such a cooperative patient. He towered over the other nestlings in the nursery but his child-like personality reminded us of his age.

His leg healed without complications. The wing was weakened by the trauma, so Crow Crow stayed in captivity much longer than usual in order to give him the physical therapy needed to see him fly one day.

A spacious cage was built for him. The many parallel perches that I put in the cage helped him to exercise both the injured leg and wing. He was in no hurry to leave his outdoor home. The creature comforts were stronger than the call of the wild. Crow Crow watched all the activity that the backyard and adjoining woods had to offer. He watched me feed the birds in the other aviaries. He watched the young squirrels in the cage by the house. The many bird feeders that hung in the trees attracted hundreds of songbirds, while the donated bread from a local bakery attracted the crows. The sanctuary was his private entertainment center.

My intention was not to keep my crow as a pet. This is the last thing that should be on the mind of a wildlife rehabilitator. In the 17-years that I have done this work, Crow Crow and two mourning doves were the only animals that imprinted on me. Considering the fact that I have cared for over 5,000 animals, I am pleased with my record.

I am sure that the reason Crow Crow decided to stay with us was because we handled him so much when he was young. His injuries forced us to give him a great deal of extra attention. The leg and wing damage forced us to keep him in confinement so that the bones could heal. When it was time to coax him to exercise, I was the one who spent hours with him.

There was something special about this crow. When it was time to give him his freedom, there was some hesitation before he flew out of the cage. The sanctuary was his home. He was set free in his own territory. As he flew around the yard, I could see the subtle bend in the wing where the fracture had healed, forming a calcium deposit. With all his energy, he cleared the trees and proudly toured the neighbor's yard. Not wanting to be out of my sight, he circled the sanctuary to let me share this moment. For nearly a year, Crow Crow had watched the other animals come and go. It saddened me to think that my healing touch had not been enough to set him free too.

"Your time will come, Crow Crow," I had promised him. Now he was flying over my head. This was a day to be joyful!

I never remember a day when Crow Crow was not here on the sanctuary. Many a friend and client stayed a little longer to enjoy his company. I always warned them not to leave anything shiny on the ground or picnic table. Crows are known for their propensity for coins, jewelry and keys.

More important to Crow Crow was his love of the birdbath that sat in the middle of our backyard. There were three other baths from which to choose, but this one was his favorite. He never took a bath unless I first changed the water. To get my attention, he stared at me as I relaxed in my recliner which faced the picture window in our family room. Sometimes he perched in a tree by the house, but usually he stood on the roof of a cage right outside the window. If I didn't get up right away, he stared at me until I did! This bird had a knack for grabbing my heart and not letting go.

As many times as I repeated the birdbath routine in the six years that he lived on the sanctuary, I always looked forward to predicting the exact movements he took to achieve the ultimate bath. After I cleaned the bowl, Crow Crow flew from his perch straight to its rim. He then jumped into the water and shook himself to dampen his feathers. He returned to the rim and jumped to the ground. To the first time observer, his bath seemed to be over. Within seconds he was in the birdbath again submerging himself until he was soaked. Was he finished? Absolutely not. Back to the ground he'd go, preening himself just long enough to prepare the feathers for another dip. This compulsion was repeated five times in total before it was time to dry out. Then he did the most amazing thing that I have ever seen. He looked around for a twig, combing the grass with his eyes. When he found one, which I assumed was just the right size, he picked it up in his beak, hopped across the yard, walked up the trunk of a leaning tree and used the twig as a balancing pole much like ones used by acrobats to keep their balance! When he reached the top branch of the tree, down came the twig after his strong legs secured his lofty position. He watched the twig as it fell to the ground. Letting the sunlight hasten his preening, he was ready to take flight again.

When the crow was wet, his wing, weakened by the fracture, prevented him from being able to fly. Once he was dry and the weight of the water had disappeared, Crow Crow resumed his normal flying habits. I wish I had a dollar for every time I made a wager with my friends that I could predict exactly what my bird was about to do as I prepared his bath. Just to see the their eyes light up was reward enough for me. Yes, this bird was truly special.

One Thanksgiving morning, the sky darkened with the coming of a flock of thousands of crows. They filled the trees of our sanctuary as though they were substitutes for the leaves that once graced their branches. We thought they would be gone in a day or two. They stayed the entire winter and spring. Crow Crow didn't seem fazed by their presence. If ever there was a time for him to join his own kind, this was it. I put out plenty of food for them. The winter set a record for snowfall that year. My time was spent driving from retailers to warehouses collecting as much food as I could to continue my mission. Crow Crow always had access to the best food in "Crow Town". He was smart enough to stay close to our picture window! He didn't take baths in the winter but he used the same tactics to get food handouts as he did to get his bath water changed.

Once spring had arrived, we prepared for the babies soon to be born. The snow had melted, but the crows were still around. Whenever a predator was on the property, we heard the loudest commotion from the flock. Their deafening screams sometimes chased the hawks or cats away. Sometimes the smaller birds were snatched and taken nearby to be finished off and eaten. Easter Sunday afternoon, after having helped Crow Crow take a bath, I came back into the house to do some work in the office. I heard the distress calls of the flock of crows coming from the school playground, a block behind and to the north of our home. Having tried to intervene on many other occasions without much success, I went back to doing my paperwork.

The next day, I noticed Crow Crow was nowhere to be found. For the first time in six years my crow was conspicuously missing. I searched the woods, hoping to find him alive, hiding in the underbrush. The long, subdued days of looking for him turned to weeks of hoping just to find his remains. Everyone tried to tell me that he had left with a female from the flock but I didn't believe them. In my heart I knew that the commotion I had heard on Easter Sunday was probably the opportunity that a hawk used to catch Crow Crow after he had taken his bath.

Crow Crow was always a big brother to the other young crows that were raised here with us. He helped us keep them wild. They imprinted on him rather than me. That was one of his special gifts.

A gift is something you give freely without any expectations in return. This book is my gift to you, Crow Crow and to all the animals whose stories must be told. For it is in these stories that lessons are learned as the chapters are read.

I believe that life should be a shared experience. The secrets of the animals were revealed to me. I, in turn, pass them on to you. Embrace them. Hold them close but only for a little while, for it is in their continued revelation that the journey will never be forgotten.

I hope you enjoyed the journey!

All proceeds generated from the

sale of this book will be used

to support the activities of

Volunteers For Distressed Wildlife.

A Song In My Heart

Whenever nature asks me in her special way.
To help the furred and feathered, I'll have one thing to say.

Dear mother of the forest, the stream, the sky, the wind.
When your children need me, I'll mend their broken limbs.
And when they're strong and healthy, please trust me when I say.
I'll give them back their freedom and set them free that day.

Creatures of the forest, I can't ignore your calls.
I'll mend your broken wings. I'll help you when you fall.
Oh creatures of the city, that once you called your home.
But man has taken acres and made them all his own.

Oh creatures of the darkness, you wake up to the night.
The owl and the fox, such beauty and such might.
You've shared with me your secrets, and one thing is for sure.
When God gave us the gifts of day, at night he gave us more.

Dear mother of the forest, the stream, the sky, the wind.
When your children need me, I'll mend their broken limbs.
And when they're strong and healthy, please trust me when I say.
I'll give them back their freedom, and set them free that day.

And when my work has ended, their dignity restored,
I know there'll be a time and place when you will ask once more.

For a cassette of this original song
Please contact
Denise Ziter at: (518) 235 - 3981

133

To order additional copies of **And Then I'll Set You Free**, complete the information below.

(please print)

Ship to: Name _____

       Address _____

       City, State, Zip _____

       Day phone _____

_____copies of **And Then I'll Set You Free.**

                   @ $ 12.95 each $ _____

     Postage and handling @ $ 2.05 per book $ _____

     Total amount enclosed $ _____

Make checks payable to: Volunteers For Distressed Wildlife

Send to:

Denise A. Ziter
Care of Volunteers for Distressed Wildlife
33 New Turnpike Rd.,
Troy, NY 12182

....

To order additional copies of **And Then I'll Set You Free**, complete the information below.

(please print)

Ship to: Name _____

       Address _____

       City, State, Zip _____

       Day phone _____

_____copies of **And Then I'll Set You Free.**

                   @ $ 12.95 each $ _____

     Postage and handling @ $ 2.05 per book $ _____

     Total amount enclosed $ _____

Make checks payable to: Volunteers For Distressed Wildlife

Send to:

Denise A. Ziter
Care of Volunteers for Distressed Wildlife
33 New Turnpike Rd.,
Troy, NY 12182